# POPULAR LEISURE
## and the
## MUSIC HALL
### in
## NINETEENTH-CENTURY
## BOLTON

by

Robert Poole

Centre for North-West Regional Studies
University of Lancaster
Occasional Paper No. 12

1982

General Editor: Oliver M. Westall

Cover: Procession in Churchgate, Bolton, in 1846. On the roof of the Star Inn can be seen the famous ship's mast, figurehead and promenade. Lined with pubs, Churchgate was already Bolton's centre of popular entertainment.

ISSN 0308-4310

ISBN 0901 699942

This volume is the twelfth in a series of occasional papers in which contributions to the study of the North West are published by the Centre for North West Regional Studies in the University of Lancaster and are available from there. The general editor will be pleased to consider manuscripts of between 10,000 and 25,000 words on topics in the natural or social sciences and humanities which relate to the counties of Lancashire or Cumbria.

PREVIOUS TITLES

*Windermere in the Nineteenth Century*
*Working Class Barrow and Lancaster 1890 to 1930*
*Handloom Weavers' Cottages in Central Lancashire*
*Flowering Plants and Ferns of Cumbria*
*Early Lancaster Friends*
*Traditional Houses of the Fylde*
*Peter Newby: 18th Century Lancashire Recusant Poet*
*North-West Theses and Dissertations 1950–1978: A Bibliography*
*Lancaster: The Evolution of its Townscape to 1800*
*Richard Marsden and the Preston Chartists, 1837–1848*
*The Grand Theatre, Lancaster: Two Centuries of Entertainment*

This publication has been supported in part by Bolton Metropolitan Borough Council, who have also allowed the use of photographs from the Local Studies Collection of its Library.

Printed in England by W. S. Maney & Son Ltd., Leeds

# CONTENTS

# Preface

All work makes Jack a dull lad, and it was surely the case that for most people in nineteenth-century Lancashire life was far more dull than it ought to have been. Yet the capacity of the factory system to squeeze work out of men and women was never as inexorable as Mr Gradgrind would have wished. Industrial workers sought as effective an escape from the tyranny of the machine as their limited incomes and spare time made possible, and their need was sufficiently great to give this search a desperate vigour.

Robert Poole has been enabled by Bolton Metropolitan Borough Council to study the ways in which people in the town enjoyed themselves outside the factory, and it has now generously helped this publication of his findings. While he touches on other groups, his main focus is on the working men and women of Bolton. Some of the traditional activities from the pre-industrial period were sustained, sometimes in modified form, but the nineteenth century saw the creation of a more organised and systematic leisure. Some was provided by those who wished to see working people become a respectable, educated and accommodating element in society, and there is little doubt that many found sober fulfilment in library and chapel. The market was also important. The demand for entertainment became a commercial opportunity seized by pubs and by the music hall which Mr Poole is able to describe in remarkable detail. Finally, there were the myriad of clubs and societies, mostly associated with sport, which working people organised for themselves, especially from the middle decades of the century, demonstrating their genius for self-imposed institutionalisation so characteristic of the period.

The material Mr Poole provides will be valuable to social historians who are becoming particularly interested in the history of leisure. Above all, it will entertain modern Boltonians who will be intrigued by the capacity for creating fun and enjoyment shown by their forbears.

Oliver M. Westall

# Acknowledgements

This study was undertaken for the first Bolton Research Award, a bursary generously financed by the then Arts Department of Bolton Metropolitan Borough from the proceeds of the municipal lottery. Thanks are due first and foremost to them for making it possible. It is to be hoped that such an enlightened venture will be repeated in future years.

The original and longer version of this book, entitled 'Leisure in Bolton, 1750–1900', is available as a typescript in Bolton Reference Library, and may soon be obtainable by inter-library loan. Many developments mentioned only briefly here are described more fully there. Much of the material relating to Bolton's theatres and music halls is also being deposited *en bloc* in the Reference Library.

I have received valuable help from many people. Particular thanks are due to John Walton, for giving freely of his time in supervising the whole project from start to finish and reading several drafts; to Kevin Campbell, the Bolton Borough archivist, for some tireless help with sources; to Barry Mills, the Bolton local history librarian, for many helpful suggestions; to all the staff in Bolton Reference Library, for putting up with me; to Margaret Elsworth, for permission to draw upon her work on physical recreation in Bolton; to Tom Dunne, for entrusting me with the final draft of his thesis on the development of libraries in Bolton; to Lesley Brain, for permission to draw upon her dissertation on leisure in Bolton between 1890 and 1914; to Peter Bailey, Kathleen Barker, Harold Perkin, Douglas Reid, Lois Rutherford and Oliver Westall, for reading and commenting upon the typescript; to Marion McClintock and Oliver Westall for helping the study towards its published form; and, of course, to Lesley, who in her many ways made the whole undertaking so much easier.

Robert Poole

# Abbreviations

*BC*: Bolton Chronicle

*B.Ex*: Bolton Express

*BEN*: Bolton Evening News

*BFP*: Bolton Free Press

*BJG*: Bolton Journal & Guardian

*BL*: Bowtun Loominary

*BRL*: Bolton Reference Library

*BWJ*: Bolton Weekly Journal

*FJ*: Farnworth Journal

*LL*: Lankishire Loominary

*PP*: Parliamentary Papers

*PRO*: Public Record Office

*Greenhalgh MSS*: Robert Greenhalgh Manuscripts (1909, in *BRL*).

# 1

# Bolton

In 1739, Daniel Defoe visited Bolton and 'saw nothing remarkable in the town, but noted that the cotton manufacture had reached it'. In 1773 Bolton was a large, straggling village of 5,339 people; the Town Hall Square was fringed with gardens and, in Little Bolton, meadows and gardens reached down to the Croal.[1] A girl born in Bolton then would have grown up in a prosperous community where handloom weaving flourished; she would have seen the riots and unrest triggered off by the French revolution and the terrible wars which followed; she would have seen the violent class struggles as the village of her youth was transformed into a great cotton town with a sky line of mill chimneys and a population of (in 1851) 61,000; and, as she sat on the doorstep of her blackened terrace where once an orchard might have stood, she would perhaps have seen the young Friedrich Engels collecting information for his angry book, *The Conditions of the Working Class in England in 1844*.

Bolton, thought Engels, was 'one of the worst' of Lancashire's industrial towns, all of which consisted of:

> Almost wholly working-people's districts, interspersed only with factories, a few thoroughfares lined with shops, and a few lanes along which the houses and gardens of the manufacturers are scattered like villas. The towns themselves are badly and irregularly built, with foul courts, lanes and back-alleys . . . Cellar-dwellings are general here . . . Bolton . . . has but one main street, a very dirty one, Deansgate, which serves as a market, and is even in the finest weather a dark, unattractive hole.[2]

The average lifespan of a gentleman was 34; of a tradesman, 23; and of workers, 18; high infant mortality partly accounts for these startling figures, but the social difference they show is even greater when it is considered that for some grades of worker, life expectation was even lower.[3] Large numbers of children worked in the cotton factories as well as wives and mothers, and until 1847 the factory acts only too often made little difference to their long hours of work. Up to 18 hours a day at the factory left people with no time in the week for leisure, and certainly no mental energy for study and 'self-improvement' so often urged upon them by others.[4] The Acts of 1847–50 limited the working week in cotton factories to ten and a half hours a day and half a day on Saturdays, but it was some twenty years before this had reached most other industries, and another twenty years before shopworkers, who still often worked twelve hours a day, got their half-holiday.

Harsh though conditions were, the Bolton of the first half of the nineteenth century was nothing like the efficiently regimented industrial cities of twentieth-century nightmares. On the contrary, it had grown up largely unplanned, and its working class once they finished work were left to their own devices. Of course, they lost a great deal to 'progress'. The magistrates and men of property had, said the *Bolton Chronicle* in 1827, as far as possible abolished those occasions of public amusement in which the people once indulged, and the extensive moors and wastelands, in which the population, particularly the younger portion, used to indulge in manly and invigorating sports, are now inclosed, and if a luckless wight ventures out of a footpath or the highway, he is liable to be prosecuted . . . Then the religious part of the community designate all outward symptoms of satisfaction, mirth, complacency, or even phlegm, as sinful, and they strenuously support the magistrates.[5]

This was a hasty generalisation, founded on some facts but written in anger. Games were still played on some enclosed parts of the moor, and on the roadways, which the tiny police force was powerless to prevent; urban growth, not prosecution, was the enemy of playfully inclined adults and children.[6] Most employers did not pretend to influence what their workers did outside the factory, except for a few masters of model factory colonies outside Bolton. The new Bolton Corporation, formed in 1839, might have helped remedy this social neglect, but it was almost paralysed for a dozen years by opposition to its very existence from conservative, often out-of-town magnates who saw the new authority as an expense and a political challenge which they had no reason to support. The 1830s and 1840s saw rapid population growth, a disastrous roller-coaster series of economic booms and slumps, the coming of steam-powered factory mechanisation on a large scale, the terrible decline of hand-loom weaving (once Bolton's staple industry, and still so for large numbers of the poor) and a great deal of radical political activity. The Chartist movement was strong in Bolton, although the existing strength of trade unionism with its more limited economic outlook helped here to blunt the movement's political edge.[7] As a result of decades of undisciplined growth Bolton became, according to a reporter for the London *Morning Chronicle* in 1849,

As bad a specimen of a nucleus of cotton manufactures as can be conceived . . . inhabited by what in this part of the country is known as an "old" population — a population which in a great degree preserves hurtful old prejudices and filthy old fashions, which have no hold in the more modern seats of industry.[8]

Around the middle of the nineteenth century, however, Bolton society noticeably settled down into a way of life which lasted, remarkably unchanged, until the outbreak of the Great War in 1914. It has been remarked that between 1850 and 1900, industrial Lancashire 'witnessed a degree of social calm perhaps unique in English industrial society'.[9] Bolton was a prime example of this.

By 1850, Bolton was a well established cotton town, one of the oldest, with a population of over 60,000. It was a centre of fine spinning, a branch of the industry which was notably immune from foreign competition, and of textile engineering, where a handful of big firms such as Dobson and Barlow predominated.[10] Half the adult population had at this time been born outside the town, but this proportion began to decline as population growth slowed, and local society took on an air of permanence. Bolton continued to grow, and the population reached 104,000 in 1877 (after the incorporation of Halliwell and Rumworth) and 141,000 in 1901, after another eleven townships had been brought within the borough. This

Fig. 1   Bolton Old Market Place, at the corner of Deansgate and Bradshawgate, in the earlier nineteenth century. The Millstone Inn, which was the home of Thomas Sharples's original Star Concert Room from 1832 to 1840, can be seen on the right.

growth, however, was anything but disruptive. Unlike the great, sprawling cities of Manchester and Liverpool, Bolton grew by 'cellular reproduction'. As it spread, it absorbed the many established and stable mill colonies around its outskirts, and at the same time retained its old, familiar town centre, small enough to walk across in a few minutes, which provided regular weekend leisure in its spacious pubs, saloons and music halls for the otherwise self-contained communities of the suburbs. In 1871, half Bolton's workforce were in factories, many of which had been established for several decades. Many more lived and worked in factory-dominated areas, in trades which depended on the custom of factories and their workers.[11] The Chartist politics of the 1840s had been superceded by the 'new model unionism' which was socially conservative, accepting the existing industrial set-up; the skilled senior workers who promoted the movement had enough social status inside and outside their workplaces for their attitudes to be shared by the community as a whole. Generations from the same family, male as well as female, followed each other into the mills. Bolton's élite of employers and gentlemen by now also had deep local roots, and was held together (economically and socially, if not politically) by a complex web of marriage and business connections which ensured that the same family names familiar among the élite of a century before still dominated the town in the 1920s.[12] The 1850s, in Bolton as elsewhere, saw the rise of a 'new paternalism': a consciousness among employers that it was in their own interests to provide their workers with housing, schools,

3

reading rooms, baths, excursions, celebration dinners, sports' facilities, brass bands and other facilities. These things were often open to workers' families and neighbours, so that the factory became the centre of the whole community. Many employers continued to live close to their workers, and even when they moved away, it was nearly always to one of the more exclusive suburbs, such as Heaton (where some of their houses can still be seen along Chorley New Road). Family members remained in charge of individual factories, and it was only in the last decade of the century that the more large and impersonal limited companies began to make any substantial inroads on this personal style of management.[13] The town council, although it remained hampered by the preference of many employers to support their own private local social provisions, began to do its bit in the 1850s and 1860s, setting up parks, libraries and the imposing town hall. The council fell under Conservative control for sixty years from 1869. Housing conditions were still often abominable, particularly in the outskirts where it had little control, and in 1871, one in twelve of the population were living in cellars, but at least councillors could always allay criticism by pointing to something that was being done.[14] In short, Bolton in the second half of the nineteenth century was one of the main centres of 'urban-industrial Toryism', where 'a high degree of union organisation and a powerful employer paternalism' produced a long period of 'industrial peace and class harmony'.[15]

This did not, however, mean that the behaviour of Bolton's people was as firmly under the control of Bolton's employers as was their environment, least of all when they were at leisure. Schemes for new types of sober, self-improving 'rational recreation' through libraries, schools, societies and institutes, attracted only a minority — ten per cent of the workforce would seem an optimistic estimate.[16] Employers' social control only worked because on the whole they refrained from trying to dictate manners and morals, but preferred to present themselves and their factories and facilities as examples of what the working man wanted — no-nonsense, hearty and sociable, with plenty of room for the individual. The traditional values and leisure preferences of Bolton's 'old' population were preserved under the wing of 'the new paternalism', and employees' compliance with the ways of their masters could still be very calculated and superficial.[17] Even where the form of leisure changed (from pub to club, for example), the substance, often alcoholic, remained similar. Popular leisure pastimes continued to outrage a large section of religious and 'improving' middle-class opinion, which included many employers when they were wearing their moralists' rather than their paternalists' hats. The real class war had been decided by 1850 when Bolton became a settled, employer-dominated industrial town, but for generations longer a phoney class war continued for the hearts and minds of the people, waged on the battlegrounds of the street, the pub and the music hall. It was probably good for the town's social stability that the reformers were soundly defeated.[18]

The story of leisure in Bolton in our period, then, is to a great extent the story of the interplay between the frustrated designs of reformers and the adaptable

4

vitality of popular pastimes. Looking below the surface of life, we find that traditional, and even pre-industrial, leisure had a profound influence over the way in which working-class social life developed.

*Notes*
1.  M. Price, "Bolton, and the Effect of the French Revolution and Napoleonic Wars 1789–1815" (Chorley College Cert. Ed. dissertation, 1972), pp. 1–3.
2.  F. Engels, *The Condition of the Working Class in England* (Panther edn., London, 1969), pp. 75–6.
3.  D. O'Connor, "Barrow Bridge" (typescript in Bolton Reference Library), p. 56.
4.  D. Gadian, "Popular Movements in North-West Towns, 1830–1850" (University of Lancaster Ph.D., 1976), p. 91; W. Dodd, *The Factory System Illustrated* (1842; rep. London, 1968), p. 63; S. Dyson, "Local Notes and Reminiscences of Farnworth" (typescript in Farnworth Library, 1894), p. 11.
5.  *BC*, 6.1.1887. Nor would anyone be surprised who had read George Vasey's 1877 masterpiece of deranged moralism, *The Philosophy of Laughter and Smiling*.
6.  See below, Chapter 2, paragraph 2.
7.  Patrick Joyce, *Work, Society and Politics: The Culture of the Factory in Later Victorian England* (Sussex, 1980), p. 57.
8.  A. B. Reach, *Manchester and the Textile Districts in 1849* (Helmshore, 1972), p. 65.
9.  Joyce, *op. cit.*, p. 90.
10.  Joyce, *op. cit.*, p. 160.
11.  Joyce, *op. cit.*, pp. 106, 118; G. Evans, "Social Leadership and Social Control in Bolton, 1870–98" (University of Lancaster M.A., 1974), pp. 17–18; E. Thorpe, "Industrial Relations and the Social Structure: a Case Study of the Bolton Cotton Spinners, 1884–1910" (University of Salford M.Sc., 1969, in Bolton Reference Library), Chapters 15–17; Gadian, thesis, Appendices 1, 2, 3 and Chapter 3.
12.  Joyce, *op. cit.*, pp. 18–20; P. Harris, "Social Leadership and Social Attitudes in Bolton, 1919 to 1939" (University of Lancaster Ph.D., 1974), Chapter 1.
13.  Joyce, *op. cit.*, pp. 59, 118–25, 172; Evans, dissertation, pp. 17–18; Harris, thesis, pp. 103–4 and Chapter 2; Thorpe, thesis, pp. 266–9; F. Baker, *The Moral Tone of the Factory System Defended* (London, 1850, in *BRL*).
14.  Evans, dissertation, pp. 18–24; Harris, thesis, p. 401.
15.  Joyce, *op. cit.*, pp. 68–9, 339; Evans, dissertation, pp. 12–13, 46.
16.  Joyce, *op. cit.*, pp. 171–2.
17.  Joyce, *op. cit.*, pp. 136–8, 148–51, 164–5, 176–9.
18.  This work thus falls somewhere between the social stability arguments of Patrick Joyce in *Work, Society and Politics*, and the arguments of continued class conflict through leisure of Peter Bailey in *Leisure and Class in Victorian England* (London, 1978), whose 'modest running case study' of Bolton provided this study with a very substantial grounding. It accords with the view of Hugh Cunningham that the first half of the nineteenth century saw 'a vigorous growth of popular leisure'. (*Leisure in the Industrial Revolution* (London, 1980), p. 9, and Chapters 1 and 2.) The evidence collected here for Bolton argues against Bailey's description of employers moving out of the area from the 1870s, and letting the older style of paternalism (Joyce's 'new paternalism') lapse (*Leisure and Class*, pp. 103–4). Joyce, however, seems to pass over the extent to which there was a culture of opposition beneath the surface conformity of the working-class to the social discipline of factory life, the expression of which opposition in popular leisure is a central theme of Bailey's book. An attempt to reconcile these is made in the conclusion.

# 2
# Old Bolton

The essence of pre-industrial leisure was that it was informal, sociable, and used plenty of space. Before the days of the factory, hours of work, though long, were much less rigid and regimented, especially for Bolton's many handloom weavers, who were their own and their family's task-masters. Like the miners in the area's scattered small collieries, they were free to observe customary holidays, whether it was 'Saint Monday' at the beginning of the week, or some annual occasion, such as New Year, Easter, Whit, some real saint's day (Saint Crispin for the cobblers), or a local wakes or fair. In good times, they could afford the time off; in bad times, they might have no work to do anyway, and as long as leisure involved little expense or preparation and much sociability, it was always welcomed. A Bolton magistrate described in 1783 how

> one evening I met a very large procession of young men and women with fiddles, garlands, and other ostentation of rural finery, dancing Morris dances in the highway merely to celebrate an idle anniversary, or what they have been pleased to call for a year or two, a fair at a paltry thatched alehouse upon the neighbouring common.[1]

Popular taste was as yet untouched by the more refined sensibilities which were spreading amongst the growing middle-class, and the pastimes at such occasions were often a riotous letting-off of steam. Cock-fighting, bull-baiting and bear-baiting were popular, while Lancashire was notorious for the practice of some of its men (notably miners) fighting to the death in iron-tipped clogs over trifling arguments. With fields or common land always close at hand, even near Bolton itself, favourite pastimes included loosely-organised games of cricket, football and knurr-and-spell, chasing games such as 'prison bars', and the hilarious 'rustic sports' staged by publicans, such as climbing the greasy pole for a leg of mutton, chasing a greased pig, and 'grinning' through a horse-collar.

All these pastimes needed space, and were in the end seriously affected by the enclosure of farmland for intensive farming or building in the late eighteenth and early nineteenth centuries. The inroads into leisure time made by factory discipline from this time were substantial, but there were in any case still plenty of people who did not work in factories to play games in the open given the chance. By 1833, the progress of enclosure and urban growth was such that, round Bolton, there were 'no public walks, or open spaces in the nature of walks, or public gardens reserved at all' for the people. Some fields were still unofficial play-grounds, with their owners turning a blind eye, but children now played on the public highways; one local MP thought that Deansgate, the street described by Engels as a 'dark and dingy hole', was perfectly adequate for this purpose.[2] Some adult sports, as well as numerous idler pastimes involving gambling, simply transferred themselves to the public highways, surviving as 'public nuisances' rather than revered 'manly sports' until well into the nineteenth century.

6

Customary pastimes, then, rather than being wiped out *en masse* along with the leisure time of their participants by the coming of the factory system, shared a variety of fates. Some, such as old-style football, in the end disappeared through lack of time and space. Some persisted, but in a less expansive form. Among the blood sports, bull and bear-baiting (which could hardly be disguised) were suppressed by the law. Cock-fighting continued for much longer in private rooms and on some gentlemen's estates. Variants such as dog-fighting, ratting and badger-fighting continued longer still, with semi-legal status, on a limited regular circuit. Some other pastimes, such as wrestling, assumed new forms and found a niche in urban society. Others still gained in popularity in the first half of the nineteenth century; this was the case with many wakes and fairs, and with the absurd pub sports, such as donkey racing and grinning through a horse collar, which developed along with the rest of pub life in the new urban environment. The old concern with animals and the countryside was also expressed in newer sports which were none the less very much products of town life, such as pigeon-fancying, dog-breeding and angling. Finally, the deep-rooted society of the pub, and the eternal popularity of gambling and betting in all their various forms, form a constant background to all working-class leisure in our period. A few examples of particular sports and pastimes will help to illustrate these themes.

Football was played in Bolton until the early 1800s, with huge disorganised teams wearing clogs surging from one end of the town centre to the other. Huge kicks were well thought of, and the ball often ended up in the Croal. Fortunately, it was often paid for by Parson Folds, a veteran local character, who would start the games himself from the yard of the old Swan Inn in Bradshawgate, booting the ball mightily backwards over his head. The complaints of local residents reached the County Court in May 1791, and the game was declared a serious breach of the peace, but this had little effect. By the time the good Parson Folds died in 1820, however, Bridson's bleachworks occupied one of the former goal areas, and the building up of the town centre in general had put a stop to football there; it was now considered to be 'too rough and uncivil a game for adults of good breeding'.[3]

Foot racing, or 'pedestrianism', which required no play area or goals, survived for much longer on the outskirts of Bolton. Local champions were attracting great crowds in the 1820s, '30s and '40s, as well as heavy backing from publicans, sporting gentlemen and gamblers. On race days, thousands would crowd the course, usually between 100 yards and a mile long. A lot of money changed hands, foul play and intimidation were not unknown, and every race was followed by a fresh challenge. Bolton's most famous 'pedestrian' was a weaver, Ben Hart, whose feats could empty the town's mills for half a day as people flocked to watch. One Monday in 1834 he raced against the famous 'mountain Stag' from Belmont, before a crowd of 5,000 on Kersal Moor, for a purse of £30, put up by rich backers. News of his victory was despatched to different places by carrier pigeon, and thousands lined Bolton's Manchester Road to await the gentleman on horse-back who was to announce the result. Ben Hart retired a rich man, to manage a pub near Rivington Pike from which he staged his own contests.[4] Race running and

Fig. 2   An outing from Bromilow's to Holcombe Hunt, 1905.

training were still common in the suburbs of Bolton in the 1860s, where the 'half-naked' state of the runners outraged middle-class residents.[5] Some races took the form of otherwise pointless feats undertaken for wagers such as pushing loaded wheelbarrows or picking up peas, and these long outlived the coming in the 1860s of formal athletics festivals with their altruistic striving for medals. Thus, in Belmont in the 1890s

> a contest was arranged between a Yorkshire terrier and a little man with a long body and very short legs, who was known as 'Wigan Bob'.

Running 200 yards to the terrier's 100, he won.[6]

Following the hunt on foot was one source of the enthusiasm for pedestrianism. In at least one Bolton mill, which backed on to fields, the workers would leave their work and give chase when the hunt came past as late as the 1850s. About this time the Holcombe hunt, whose run went past Bolton, was having a crisis of membership and influence. They lost their permission to run over part of the area when a local landowner complained of working-class foot followers breaking down fences. They survived the decade, however (unlike the neighbouring Bury Hunt), and although they stopped advertising their starting points in the local press in the 1840s, they kept up their working-class contact until 1884 by organising the trail hunt at the annual Holcombe Wakes.[7]

8

Pigeon-flying was a pre-industrial pastime which came into its own in industrial Bolton and remained popular throughout the nineteenth century. It was (like many working-class pastimes) regarded as disreputable because it usually happened on Sundays — the only full spare day most working men had during the week — and because of its association with pubs and betting. The Farnworth constable in the 1820s would spend his Sunday mornings rounding up offenders and shutting them (and sometimes their pigeons) in the church's box pews. The sport became very popular among the Bolton youth, who would 'carry on a system of endeavouring to entice and entrap each other's stock, and conduct it more as a system of plunder than otherwise', hurling stones over the rooftops at the birds, to the great annoyance of passers-by on the other side. The coming of the railway gave pigeon-flying a new lease of life as an adult sport. Enthusiasts (often railway guards) could carry birds to distant destinations to be released, and pigeon flying became a highly-organised pub-based sport, described in all its subtle colour by Mass Observation in the 1930s. It was — and is — taken very seriously; there is one story that a party of enthusiasts held up a funeral cortege while a pigeon passed over, in case the movement should confuse its flight path![8]

Fishing was another sport given a boost by the railways, which enabled anglers to gather for competitions on favourable stretches of water all over the county. There was some continuity from earlier decades, for some streams close to Bolton remained fishable in the 1820s and 1830s, and many moorland streams within walking distance remained unpolluted. The boom in the popularity of angling came in the 1860s. Angling contests offered a vast army of useful material prizes — kettles, snuff boxes, mugs and so on — in contrast with the sports festivals at the same time, where the organisers clearly preferred cups, medals and other abstract orders of merit as less of an incentive to cheating, gambling and gamesmanship. When Mass Observation arrived in Bolton in the 1930s, they found that angling still had pub connections and a strong element of betting and cunning.[9]

The popularity of fighting and trials of strength was preserved in the form of wrestling, the modern, respectable successor of pugilism. Wrestling in the Cumbrian style was introduced to Bolton in 1844 at a public sports' match organised by 'a number of respectable gentlemen in the town' who, it was reported, 'aim entirely at displaying strength and energy in the field of conflict, and utterly despise and reject all the blackguardism connected with what is politely called the customs of "The Ring"'. This was in accord with the new respectable values of 'rational recreation', but wrestling had a reputable following in Bolton before the Cumbrian rules were introduced: Robert Lord, a Farnworth millowner, would parade the street in his singlet at the annual wakes, challenging people to wrestle him. This highlights the dual class appeal of the sport, and it caught on amongst the working-class as a skilful recreation, but within the same pub and betting milieu that surrounded foot-racing. Men who might have learnt to wrestle in the 1840s were still passing on their skills to the youth of Kearsley at the turn of this century.[10]

Boxing never caught on in the same way in Bolton, probably because it was too identified with the old sporting gentry who had left town society by the middle of the century, and with 'the barbarous custom' of fighting to the finish with iron-tipped clogs which often resulted in serious injury and even death. This was 'gradually disappearing' by the 1830s, giving way to organised prize fighting and the occasional exhibition of 'sparring'. The *Bolton Chronicle* applauded these 'fair and manly' contests, but prize fights were banned under the 1843 Improvement Act and the authorities broke up gatherings whenever they could. Even the *Bowtun Loominary*, usually a friend to popular amusements, attacked the 'set o cooas, low vulgar animals' and the 'bettin-men, drunkards, blackguards, prostitutes, thimble-riggers un foak uv aw shades o questionable karrickter' who frequented fights.[11]

Blood sports underwent a similar gradual decline. Bull baiting was banned in Britain in 1835, and seems to have died out in Bolton well before then, although Bolton people were still going to the bull-baits at Chowbent Wakes in the 1840s.[12] Cock-fighting was longer tolerated and less easily prevented. It was banned by the Corporation in 1843 and the Government in 1849, but it remained popular among the working-class and many conservative gentlemen for much longer, gathering a covert 'fraternity' linked with those of other towns such as Blackburn, Salford and Haslingden. James Greenhalgh later remembered how a party carrying cocks to an illegal fight disguised themselves as a funeral cortege, and how the spectators included 'local gentry', 'magistrates', manufacturers, a vicar and the police inspector 'to guard against the possible intrusion of a more than usually honest policeman'. There were allegations in 1869 that some of the town's Sabbatarian lobby attended cockfights, and a local gentleman was prosecuted for holding a cockfight in the grounds of Hulton Hall in 1925; the sport is still rumoured to survive in the remoter parts of the north-west.[13]

Dog-fighting did not similarly benefit from upper-class patronage, but it survived none the less into the 1860s and probably beyond on the ill-policed outskirts of Bolton. When police broke up a midnight dog-fight in a field at Horwich, there were spectators from all over Lancashire, but the most they could do was fine a handful of them three-halfpence each for damaging the field.[14] Bolton also had at least two rat pits around the middle of the century (in Chapel Street and in Spring Garden, now Le Mans Crescent), where dogs would be set on rats to see how many they could kill in a minute. The pastime seems to have evaded legal control, but it was nothing like as popular as it was in London and little is known about it for this area.[15]

George Gray, a local music hall manager, observed in 1853 that 'the taste for brutal sports, prize fights, bull fights, and others of a like debasing tendency, has very much decreased', a view confirmed by other commentators over the previous twenty years or so.[16] The once generally popular sports were now pursued by a diminishing covert fringe of enthusiasts, which became all the more marginal with the development of other recreations from the middle of the century. The wakes and fairs where bull-baits and cockfights had once been the central attractions continued, however, undiminished, adapting smoothly to the limitations and opportunities of urban life.

A wakes was a church festival, mediaeval in origin, held to mark the day of a church's dedication to its patron saint. Wakes became firmly established as local feasts and holidays, and where there was no church, or wakes, a fair served as a holiday instead. The growth of population in the Bolton area during the Industrial Revolution brought an increase in the popularity and even the number of wakes and fairs, despite the loss of open spaces and traditional sports, and despite the opposition of the many such as Thomas Brodbelt, the 'High Priest of Ebenezer Chapel', who wrote in 1829:

> I have no hesitation in stating, in the most deliberate manner, that there is nothing which is, in any degree, so generally and practically injurious to the minds, morals, and habits of the population, and consequently to the peace, order, and happiness of the community, as the Wakes which are held in this neighbourhood; I allude to what are called Dean Church Wakes . . . They begin with an open, avowed, unblushing *profanation of the Lord's Day*. Excess, riot, and profligacy occur in many instances before the Sabbath is over . . . How many young persons have to date their ruin to the temptations which these seasons set in their way? Many people go with the full intention of being intoxicated . . . will the Vicar and Parishioners of Dean suffer such vile importers of iniquity to disgrace the parish, and spread abroad their pestilential contagion also? Shall we not rather rise up as one man, oppose and crush them . . . And ought not the Magistrates and Civil authorities to interfere?

These strictures had little effect, and the police seem to have been essentially powerless; attempting to quell a riot at Dean Wakes in 1841 they were driven off and 'obliged to take flight and bolt across the fences with more than usual alacrity'. The wakes was still held on 'charity sermons Sunday' until the 1860s or 1870s:

> Early in the afternoon of Wakes Sunday, stalls sprang up with amazing rapidity all along the lane from Cannon Street to Deane Church. Barrel organs, Aunt Sally stalls of every description, rifle ranges, ice cream carts, oyster sellers, men with travelling ovens roasting potatoes and cooking peas, dark-eyed Italian girls with gaily-coloured clothes, and handkerchiefs tied on their heads, telling fortunes with their birds; a drove of donkeys for the races, and in the public-houses an abundance of beer.

Games and races took place in the street, organised by a publican ('Owd Woof') who offered copper kettles and clothes as prizes for the fastest riders of donkeys between his pub and Dean Church:

> In the evening the unholy traffic began . . . The strident cries of the fair men, the shrieks of excited laughter from the young people, the tunes being ground out of the barrel organs, the bawls of drunken men . . . the glare of paraffin lamps, the braying of the donkeys; all made an indescribable discord.

The sight of their treasured Sunday scholars 'waltzing around and singing profane songs' was too much for the teachers of Gate Pike Sunday School, and they began an annual Wakes Monday tea party which, far from supplanting the wakes for the children, soon became a valued part of it.[17]

Among the new festivals begun in the early nineteenth century were Farnworth Wakes, which began in 1827 after the new church was built, and Cross Keys Fair,

Fig. 3 Shooting gallery at Farnworth Wakes, 1902. Farnworth Wakes was started as 'Halshaw Moor Wakes' by a local publican to mark the opening of the new Farnworth Church in 1827. The church had nothing to do with the wakes and often campaigned against it, but it was still going strong at this time.

begun by a publican in the 1800s and ending in the 1840s. The several pub-inspired holiday occasions begun in this period did not survive the middle of the century, thanks to stricter licensing requirements and loss of space, but Farnworth Wakes was still the biggest local holiday and fair in 1900. Others still then surviving as major fairs and/or holidays included Bolton New Year Fair, Bolton Whit Fair, Rivington Pike Fair at Easter and Whitsun, Turton Fair, Streetgate Wakes and Westhoughton Wakes (the 'Pasty-eating' or 'Keaw Yed' Wakes described by Mass Observation). Population growth and migration to the towns made wakes and fairs more important than ever as occasions for visits and family reunions, while the huge success of the cheap railway excursion after 1850 modernised them and ensured their continuing popularity. Many smaller local celebrations suffered eventually from the resulting exoduses, although the larger fairs, such as those in Bolton and Turton, simply widened their catchment area and went from strength to strength. Among the festivals which no longer survived in any notable way by 1900 (with the rough date of demise, where known, in brackets) were: Bolton Easter Fair, Bolton July Fair (both still existing, but without substantial pleasure fairs or any associated holiday), Cross Keys Fair (1840s), Blackrod Fair (declined

12

towards the end of the nineteenth century), Tong Fold Fair (1850s), Chowbent Wakes (1870s), Radcliffe Races (some time after 1862), Belmont Fair (about 1880), Bradshaw Wakes (another pub fair, ending before 1850), Flash Fair (existing in connection with a pub from 1808–29), Horwich Races (existing from 1837 to 1847), Holcombe Wakes (moved to Ramsbottom in the 1870s), Little Hulton Wakes (1870s) and Dean Church Wakes (last heard of in 1866). Some surviving fairs were 'civilised' by the authorities after 1850: at Rivington Pike's unofficial Easter fair, which once attracted 'the concentrated terror of a mighty district . . . harmonising in only its most dangerous proclivities', the drinksellers and stall holders were suppressed by the magistrates. The inhabitants of Tong Fold and Turton lost their customary right to sell intoxicating drinks all day during the fairs some time during the 1850s, although in the latter case this was only at the expense of licensing dozens of non-local drinksellers who had earlier been subject to futile bans. Turton Fair had been denounced as early as 1789 in a long poem (dedicated to the Manchester Inspector of Excise) by William Sheldrake, a local manufacturer of doggerel:

> This little village of such vast renown,
> Is only four miles North of BOLTON town,
> Yet, 'tis a well-frequented little place,
> Where various useful arts of late increase:
> . . . Thirteen stately houses are the most,
> Of which the great inhabitants can boast;
> Although this village only now contains
> One public alehouse for the hopeful swains;
> Each cottage is made an inn, and I'll make bold,
> To say much liquor out of doors is sold.
> But no pretender to the thirst of gain,
> Makes such advance as the village swain
> Of TURTON's inn, — he purely keeps an house
> The seasons empty, solely to carouse
> At this dread fair . . .
> This fair begins the fourth day of September,
> (Which baneful day I ever shall remember) . . .

He went on, in some 700 lines of verse, to decribe the showmen, sharks and charlatans who visited the fair, but despite his strictures it was still there in 1844, described by the *Bolton Chronicle* thus:

The sound of a "nogging" (clog) was not to be heard throughout the dense crowd; all were shod for the occasion in brand new dancing-pumps; a single note from a fiddle congregated them together in their hundreds, and they danced like automauts to any tune attempted by the most miserable scraper of "cat-gut". There were not many exhibitions of a wonderful character in the fair; there were a few "galanty shows" discribed as "most wonderful and vastly astonishing views of the battle of Vaterloo;" "her Majesty riding in state," "the pictures of the mighty Duke of Vellington and Bonaparte," "Guy Faux a-goin' to blow up the Houses of Parliament," and other

13

"mighty wonders never seen in this vold afore, and all for one halfpenny". Dancing was kept up until a late hour, and more good humour prevailed at this occasion than at previous fairs; for we did not hear that anyone suffered at Turton as they usually do at Eccles wakes, where they "settle their mouths wi' their clogs".

Like other fairs, Turton was also an occasion when young people came to find a sweetheart, but it was especially notorious for its gambling swindlers and pickpockets, who were only very gradually eliminated during the later part of the century.[18]

While pub society provided a ready home for many working-class pastimes, and the wakes and fairs provided occasional periods of licence, many other recreations spilled over into the streets, where they attracted the protests both of respectable residents and the Sabbatarian lobby. For much of the century, Sunday was the only day which most working people had free for recreation, and very few went to church. It was on Sunday that drinking, and all the other popular pastimes so deplored by moral reformers, were at their most widespread, and their most intolerable. Sunday was the one day when most respectable citizens had to go into the town centre, to worship; it was then that they saw how well the police were doing their job; it was then that they came into contact with the otherwise deferential common people on their own territory; and it was then, while working themselves into a suitably elevated state of mind, while dressed in their Sunday best, while proceeding in family groups and while at their most correct and virtuous, that they came to experience the sights, sounds and smells of a working-class left to its own devices — to be abused, mocked and spat on; to hear curses and blasphemies; to be forced off the pavement by groups of idlers and prostrate drunks into pools of mud, horse-dung and vomit; to catch sight of men relieving themselves against walls from the products of the beerhouse and the hush shop; to encounter men and boys playing pitch and toss in the street; to witness the clamour and violence of a fight between two men, or even two women; and to have to dodge balls, sticks and other missiles launched waywardly in the air by juveniles who were at play and should have been at Sunday school. Not all these things would have been seen on a typical Sunday, but they all happened, and they demonstrated the difference between the 'two nations', stirring up passions quite absent from other areas of middle-class life.[19] Many complaints give the impression that the complainants felt themselves under siege; here was the 'phoney war' between the classes in Victorian Britain. The clash between these mundane perceptions and the widespread belief in the moral and civil benefits of industrial progress perhaps explains in part the elusive and double-sided psychology of the Victorian middle-class, and also provides an essential background for our understanding of the movement for 'rational recreation'.

14

*Notes*
1. B. T. Barton, *Historical Gleanings of Bolton and District* (Bolton, 1881), p. 263, quoted in E. P. Thompson, *The Making of the English Working Class* (Penguin edn., 1968), pp. 444–5.
2. Select Committee on Public Walks, *Parliamentary Papers* 1833 xv, evidence of William Bolling, pp. 55–9.
3. Robert Greenhalgh, manuscripts (1909; in Bolton Reference Library, henceforth 'Greenhalgh MSS'); J. D. Greenhalgh, *Sayings and Doings of Parson Folds* (Bolton, 1879), p. 33; Lancashire County Quarter Sessions Papers, May 1791.
4. *BC* 22.5.1841, 19.2.1831, 4.10.1834, 1.11.1834, 15.11.1834.
5. Bailey, *op. cit.*, pp. 83–4; *BC* 17.3.1866.
6. *BC* 8.5.1841, 11.9.1841; C. M. Trevor, "History of Belmont" (MS in Bolton Reference Library), pp. 63–4.
7. W. P. Crankshaw & A. Blackburn, *A Century and a Half of Cotton Spinning* (Bolton, n.d. 1947), p. 18; A. N. Walker, *History of the Holcombe Hunt* (Manchester, 1937), pp. 111, 117; *BJG* 3.10.1905.
8. B. T. Barton, *History of Farnworth and Kearsley* (Bolton, 1887), pp. 157–9; *BC* 27.4.1844, 2.11.1850, 30.11.1850, 17.5.1851, 21.5.1852; W. Haslem, "Our Lancashire Village" (typescript in Farnworth library, *c.*1957), p. 116; Mass Observation, *The Pub and the People* (1943; repr. Welwyn, 1970), p. 291.
9. C. G. Hampson, *150th Anniversary of Robert Fletcher and Son Ltd.* (Bolton, 1973), p. 13; Crankshaw and Blackburn, *op. cit.*, p. 18; Haslam, *op. cit.*, p. 115; *Pub and the People*, pp. 291–4.
10. *BC* 3.7.1875, 20.7.1844, 21.9.1844; *FJ*, 15.6.1923; Haslam, *op. cit.*, p. 117.
11. James Black, *A Medico-Topographical, Geological and Statistical Sketch of Bolton and Its Neighbourhood* (Bolton, 1837), pp. 67–8; *BFP* 12.3.1836, 31.3.1839; *BC* 29.10.1831; *BL*, XII (1860), pp. 89–91.
12. *BC* 11.9.1841, 23.9.1843, 28.9.1850.
13. *BJG* 13.4.1928, p. 7; *BL* II (1852–3), pp. 307–8; *BL* III (1853), pp. 131–3; *BJG* 13.5.1927.
14. *BC* 18.6.1853.
15. *BJG* 1.3.1929.
16. Select Committee on Public Houses, *Parliamentary Papers* 1852–3, p. xxxvii, Q. 7781.
17. H. Cottrell, *Gate Pike* (Bolton, 1924), pp. 58–62; Greenhalgh MSS; *BC* 8.9.27, 22.9.27 (for a satirical sketch of Thomas Brodbelt), 13.9.1834, 11.9.1841.
18. W. Sheldrake, *A Picturesque Description of Turton Fair and Its Pernicious Consequences* (London, 1789); *BC* 7.9.1844, 21.9.1844, and annually; L. Knowles, *An Abstract of the Records of the Manor Court of Turton* (privately printed, Rochdale, n.d. (1909)), p. 234.
19. For further elaboration, see the section on 'Unreformed Working Class Leisure' in the longer version of this work, pp. 23–6; and Bailey, *op. cit.*, p. 21.

# 3
# New Bolton

## The Middle-Class Ideal: Recreation and Self-Improvement

Mention the word 'leisure' to anyone in early nineteenth-century Bolton and they would immediately have thought of the social round of the gentry. Bolton at this time was a centre of 'county society' — a leisured élite who regularly met each other in an endless round of land and business dealings, balls, coming-out parties, race meetings, hunts and shoots. Many of the builders of Bolton's new industry had family, land or commercial ties with the existing gentry, and shared their recreational tastes. In the French Wars and afterwards, when Bolton was (according to E. P. Thompson) perhaps 'the most insurrectionary centre in England', various 'patriotic societies' were set up to preserve the existing order. At the Church and King Club, the wealthy members met at high-class inns to dine, make loyal toasts, swap information about working-class subversives and crow over the Peterloo Massacre. In the twenty or so years after 1815, the town's role as a centre of county society diminished and it acquired its own social institutions: Little Bolton Town Hall (1828) and the Baths Assembly Rooms (1846) for large gatherings; subscription libraries, where members could meet, talk quietly and read in comfort; and numerous social and debating societies. Bolton remained a stronghold of Freemasonry. However, the growing industrial and social life of the town produced a middle-class of business and professional people, Liberals rather than Conservatives in politics and on the whole Nonconformist rather than Church of England in religion, who had their own views on leisure and who developed their own parallel social life.

Bolton's Conservative society was little more than an urban extension of the hunting, shooting and cockfighting world of county society, and its members were often to be heard proclaiming the virtues of the Englishman's roast beef and his beer. They tended to favour drinking, prize-fighting, blood sports and all sorts of revels as ways of stiffening the national fibre, keeping a disorderly people happy, and bringing the upper and lower classes together in common enjoyment — a sort of social safety valve. To Liberal reformers, the very idea of encouraging such wasteful indulgence was repellent. Strongly influenced by Nonconformist religion, they stressed that leisure should not involve squandering time, money or energy. Rather, it should involve relaxing and recuperating from work, perhaps through quiet family evenings, an invigorating walk amongst the things of nature, or some quiet and serious study, so that the mind and body were rejuvenated for further work. The *Bolton Bee*, a local magazine of 1851 dedicated to moral improvement, set forth this view with a decidedly religious gloss:

> The majority spend their leisure in sloth, sensual gratification and frivolity . . . But he that views life as a probation for another state of existence, and considers its brevity and uncertainty, will not fritter away even the moment of relaxation in indolence and folly.

16

He will seek rest rather in change of employment than in cessation of action, and thus render every part of his life in some measure subservient to the purpose of his being.[1]

Such perceptions among business and professional people owed a great deal to the uncertainty and insecurity of their own lives. This was a period when the carefully built home life of middle-class families often seemed in danger of being over-whelmed by the turbulent perils of an industrial society in the making, such as bankruptcy, loss of a vital but often precariously maintained 'respectable' stand-ing, and the epidemic diseases which were rife in the crowded town. Hard work and careful habits were a psychological as well as a financial defence. They also gave a gratifying sense that all this effort was directed towards the advancement of civilisation and morality, and not simply towards personal gain.

The same Liberal-Tory split which hampered the growth of local government in Bolton also damaged its middle-class social life. Since even basic public buildings were lacking in the early nineteenth century, setting up any new venture required support from at least some of Bolton's wealthy Tories. This was often not forthcoming. In 1824, a number of members of the exclusive Commercial Inn newsroom, who disliked its Conservative tendencies, left in order to raise money to build a more public and 'non-political' Exchange Newsroom and Library. This suffered from the defection of conservative members — some of them complain-ing that *The Times* was much too subversive to be seen in a respectable institution — who supported the vicar's successful attempt to set up a rival 'Church and King' newsroom and library. (The handsome Exchange building still survives in the Town Hall Square, occupied by the Nationwide Building Society.) In the follow-ing years, attempts to extend the idea of educational leisure to the working-class met with similar difficulties. The Mechanics' Institute of 1825 was completely boycotted by many conservatives, while a plan for an Athenaeum in 1846 was effectively sabotaged by the conservative faction led by the vicar, who refused to accept any form of education which did not conform to Church of England doctrine (see below). Political division killed two early attempts to provide the town with a park. A whole string of choral societies and glee clubs were split and destroyed by political argument, despite the growing number of music shops and teachers catering for all sections of the middle-class. Nevertheless, by the 1840s a clearly-defined middle-class society had developed, based around the dissenting chapels, the teetotal society (formed in 1833), the Exchange Newsroom (1827), the patrons of the Mechanics' Institute (1825), the entertainments at Little Bolton Town Hall (1828), the new Temperance Hall (1844) and the Baths' Assembly Rooms (1846), the fitful singing societies and social and discussion groups such as Robert Heywood's Delta Society and, on the fringe of respectability, the amateur dramatic society. All of these activities conformed with the idea that leisure should be decent, moderate, and acquisitive.

The working-classes generally neither had nor needed the sort of sense of mission in life to which the gospel of leisure through self-improvement appealed. Such efforts held out little prospect of achieving any radical improvement in the condition of life. The last thing most people wanted after a week of deadening toil was a weekend of self-restraint and disciplined study. The middle class may have needed a new set of social institutions, but the working class already had its pubs. Saturday night and Sunday were times of intense release and sociability. Nevertheless, a minority of working people, including many Chartists, did come to believe that they could improve themselves, and even their whole class, and taught themselves reading, writing, science, natural history, music and classics. Their achievements, coming on top of long hours of work, seem remarkable today.

The earliest facilities for working-class recreation and self-improvement were provided by a handful of local millowners who took it upon themselves to provide more for their workers than just a weekly wage, and incidentally to steer them towards the ways of improvement. Factory labour was initially destructive of leisure because of its long hours and enervating effects. The working week in cotton mills was not made regular until 1847–50, and other industries had to wait much longer. Well before this time, however, the Bolton area was noted for its model factory colonies: Eagley Mills, Dean Mills (Barrow Bridge) and Henry Ashworth's mills at Turton and Egerton. Ashworth's enterprises provide an interesting example.

On the one hand, Ashworth was notorious for his severe discipline, his inflexible doctrine of profit-seeking, his discarding of 40-year-old workers as 'old people', and his resistance to the compulsory education provisions of the 1833 Factory Act. On the other hand, he provided his mills from the 1820s with gardens, schoolrooms, libraries and newspaper reading rooms, and with washing rooms for adults and children so that they could clean up and use the facilities straight after work. While Ashworth's workplace regime was almost feudal, he consciously avoided dictating the morals and politics of his workforce, trusting in the power of enlightenment, and nothing (apart from work) was compulsory. The workers were 'Chartists in politics and Nonconformists in religion', and defended the mill from the radical 'Plug Riots' of 1842. As a Quaker, Ashworth believed in individual freedom of conscience; as a laissez-faire economist he believed that 'progress' was inevitable. Thus, later in life, he could happily make compromises with his landed background by drawing heavily on his profits to finance foreign holidays and shooting expeditions. He saw his basic role not as enforcing progress, but as providing the conditions for it, and had great faith in the 'perservering intelligence and industry' of 'the common man'. When there were riots at his New Eagley Mills in 1830 he simply 'had the damage repaired and endeavoured to increase the efficiency of the education'. Here was the gospel of inevitable progress at its most confident.[2]

Dean Mills, in the factory village of Barrow Bridge, was also seen as a model for the communities of the future, where work and leisure, employer and workman, were united in the pursuit of progress. Its facilities were similar to those at Turton and New Eagley, and were enhanced by the addition of the Barrow Bridge Institute in 1846, made famous by the visit of Prince Albert in 1850. Eagley Mills also had a school, library and newsroom by the 1830s, as well as a bowling green, a cricket field and, soon after, a brass band.[3] Such mill colonies earned praise even from critics of the factory system. Our view of them seems to come largely from enthusiastic reporters and carefully-staged opening ceremonies and celebrations; in fact, only a minority of workers turned to self-improvement, even when the facilities were on their doorstep. The Dean Mills Mutual Improvement Society, for example, intended as the living heart of the famous Barrow Bridge colony, disappeared in the mid-1850s through lack of support. Even when re-founded in 1863 by a new owner, W. R. Callender of Manchester (a Conservative who well understood that 'drunken men make very indifferent workmen'), its membership remained at a disappointing sixty or so, and courses of lectures in the thousand-seat lecture hall had to be abandoned.[4]

From one point of view these provisions did as much for their employers as for their workforce, who were doubtless in no state after a long day of repetitive labour to start exerting their minds. Laying on facilities for workers' self-improvement was an important way in which millowners were able to see themselves as providers, rather than as exploiters, as the improvers rather than the architects of the terrible urban conditions around them. By aiming to provide (after the manner of Ashworth) the conditions for improvement, rather than accepting responsibility for education, employers could lay the blame for the general lack of 'moral advancement' on the individual failings of workers who did not take advantage of what (however unrealistically) was offered, rather than on their own failure as employers and governors to compensate for the social damage done by the factory system. (A similar attitude was implicit in the way temperance reformers approached social problems by concentrating on individual morals rather than on the social causes of alcoholism.) The ideal of progress through profit remained intact, despite the clear failure of profit to bring about the much-heralded 'advance of civilisation'.

There was, however, an alternative philosophy behind providing amusements for workers. Tory paternalism, embodying something like a country squire mentality towards the pleasures of the poor and their place in the world, was strong in Bolton. Thus, the Conservative bleacher, Joseph Ridgway of Horwich, marked a family success by laying on a dinner for his workers at three local pubs, after which they trooped over to his residence and cheered him heartily, passing the rest of the evening 'with the utmost hilarity'. Occasions such as these were said to provide 'feelings of harmony and pleasure . . . which lasted for months' between masters and men.[5] The emphasis was on common pleasures within the social order, rather than on moralising and improving. This sort of social conservatism, applied to factory life, was to prove very important in the development of Bolton. Nevertheless, until the 1850s, most employers, Liberals and Tories alike, continued to believe that the worker should be left to his or her own devices out of working hours.

The other early promoters of 'improving' recreations were the Sunday schools. These began in Bolton in the 1780s and the demand for them was such that by 1834 nearly all working-class children were on the roll of one or another. They saw

19

Fig. 4   St. Peter's and St. Paul's Schools' Catholic Walking Day, Great Moor Street, Bolton, around 1900. Cloth caps and bowlers, berets and boaters; everyone seems to clamour for a sight.

themselves not just as schools but as straight competitors for the children's souls and leisure time with pubs, music halls, wakes, fairs and the grubby attractions of the streets. Accordingly, they began to organise picnics, outings, field days (often at the homes of wealthy patrons), Whit walks and later railway excursions, as well as the perennial tea parties (although some Wesleyans still saw beer as an acceptable childrens' drink in the mid-1830s).[6] There was a genuinely popular element in all this. There was also a progressive, almost revivalist vision which saw the Sunday schools as bringing up the first generations of the new industrial society in the ways of religion and righteousness. Unfortunately for these far-sighted optimists, the Sunday schools fitted all too smoothly into working-class life. For parents, the most popular thing about them, as well as the literacy they provided, was that they got the children out of the way on Sunday to allow, amongst other things, a little sexual privacy in overcrowded housing. For the children, the entertainments were the schools' best attraction (rolls would swell visibly before an annual treat), and as they grew up, they simply discarded them for more exciting activities. Fifty years later the Sunday schools were trying to wean the grandchildren of their first generation of scholars from the ways of their elders, and had notched up decades of campaigning against the same pitfalls.

Bolton was slow to develop public institutions of all sorts, and provision for working-class recreation suffered accordingly. Church and conservative opposition was one factor. Ironically, another may have been the way in which the progressive owners of out-of-town factory colonies apparently preferred to

20

concentrate on providing for their own workers rather than assisting developments in the nearby borough. Bolton's leading civic improver was Robert Heywood, whose bleachworks do not seem to have been distinguished by any provisions for leisure. In the long run, however, perhaps the most important drawback was lack of popular support.

The Mechanics' Institute movement of the 1820s 'represented the first try (though not the first failure) to moralise the working-classes by combining instruction with amusement'.[7] Bolton's was founded by middle-class patrons in 1825, in small premises in Back King Street. The object was to provide rooms, a library, lectures and evening classes to encourage working men to educate themselves, particularly in technical subjects which would benefit their work. To one early supporter, the Institute heralded 'that glorious and universal reign of knowledge which will, at no distant day, extend itself over the whole of Europe'. Politics and religion were banned, part of a general rule designed to make the institute as widely acceptable as possible, but even the general aim of transforming the working-class was not acceptable to many potential Conservative patrons. Fiction was also kept out of the library (although the rule was later relaxed to allow certain 'classics') because, it was believed, reading it

> would soon result in the inevitable consequence of unnatural excitment, debility and disgust . . . Works of the imagination should be read as relaxation only, as amusements after severe study, and even then, unless they are written with good taste and good feeling, they may commit infinite mischief.

Not surprisingly, then, tired workers preferred the warmth and company of the pub to the 'dull, cold, cheerless rooms of the institute'. The membership from the start was dominated by middle-class 'honorary members', tradesmen and clerks, and the few dozen working men who joined were always the first to let their membership lapse when economic depression came.[8]

In 1840 a group of Bolton Chartists founded their own more political institute, although it was still stocked with 'improving' literature and supported by 'Liberal gentlemen'. It was seen as an alternative to entertainments at pubs such as the Star. It does not seem to have lasted long.[9]

In 1846, Robert Heywood led an attempt to set up an Athenaeum or 'Institute for Popular Education' in Bolton, which would be used by all classes and succeed where the mechanics' institute had failed. It would be based on the famous Manchester Athenaeum,

> in which classes, lectures, soirees and conversaziones, musical entertainments and other attractions may be combined to offer the young men, and others of the town, occupations for their leisure hours, of a truly elevating moral and social character.

In the words of the scheme's only major Tory patron, the cotton spinner John Hick,

> An Athenaeum would afford a neutral ground where every shade of opinion, and every grade in life, might assemble for mutual good. The institution would also have a tendency to promote a better feeling between masters and their men.[10]

Like the mechanics' institute, however, the scheme failed to get Tory support, which this time proved fatal. The Vicar, as we have seen, would only support 'education conducted upon a religious [i.e. Anglican] principle', while other critics saw such institutions as

> giving many young men views and ideas not suited for their stations in life and filling their heads with vanity and self importance and unsuiting them for their daily duties of drudgers, an occupation that the mass of mankind are destined to undergo.

The Vicar instead launched an appeal for a 'Church Eductional Institution' which succeeded, maintaining its sectarian separateness even after the mechanics' institute became absorbed into the Technical College at the end of the century.[11]


## The 1850s: A New Start

After the middle of the century, once working-class radicalism had collapsed, middle-class town society, which had probably always been closer together socially than political divisions seem to indicate, became more settled and unified in its outlook. Social developments assumed a common form as formally constituted societies became the vehicle for all sorts of activities. The 1850s saw the establishment of several 'mutual improvement societies' in connection with various churches. In the 1860s and 1870s, scientific societies, and church choral societies (which must have done much to further informal inter-denominational links and thus increase the gap between the godly and the ungodly) grew up. In 1865 a scheme for a town Gentlemen's Club was mooted, an avowedly patrician idea which seemed to catch the mood of the times. It was proposed that Bolton's now extensive ruling class could meet amicably to discuss problems and settle differences, and generally 'keep the social machinery running smoothly'. The scheme failed, and Bolton's wealthy Tories went off to build themselves a luxurious Venetian gothic style Conservative club at a cost of nearly £10,000, complete with rooms for reading, writing, smoking, playing cards, playing billiards (three tables) and, of course, dining.[12] The middle class continued to be catered for by the growing network of local Liberal and Conservative clubs, which was later extended to the working class. Thus, although the political division of Bolton's middle-class continued, a social network similar on both sides was emerging.

As the opposing world views of Bolton's Liberals and Conservatives moved together, so did their attitudes towards working-class leisure. Conservatives, now more familiar with the mechanics of industrial discipline, came to the view that sobriety, thrift and some sort of self-improvement were desirable in a workforce, while Liberals came to realise that moral exhortation alone would not attract people to the way of reform; something more lively was needed. As Chartism disappeared as a political movement, working-class reformers came to favour individual self-improvement rather than class elevation, a trend given a great boost by the publication of Samuel Smiles's popular book, *Self Help*, in 1859. This change of emphasis made the idea of 'improvement' for the masses more acceptable to the many Tories who believed that, whatever individuals might achieve, the working class as a whole should stay in its place.

Although the *Bolton Chronicle* could complain in 1854 that 'the majority of employers concern themselves only to see that their operatives do their allotted work', in the 1850s and 1860s a number of local factory owners, both Liberal and Tory, followed the pioneering example of the early factory colonies and set up reading rooms, libraries and institutes for their workers; 'the new paternalism' became widely established.[13] The Great Exhibition of 1851 in London had done much to produce a consensus on ideas of national pride, progress and improvement, and it was followed by an imitation 'Factory Operatives' Exhibition' in Bolton in 1852. Although most of the exhibits were produced as a result of special encouragement, or even financial incentives, from employers, it gave a boost to the idea of allowing employees the means of useful recreation. The following wave of mill institutions gradually converged in their cultural style, expressed most clearly through the ubiquitous annual dinners, where toasts were usually given to Queen, country, prosperity, employer and factory. By 1870, many mills also had cricket and bowls facilities. Like chess boards and other indoor games, these might be attached to institutes (rather than being freely available for all employees) to act as incentives for workers to join up and pursue mental as well as physical self-improvement. Only a minority did so. As a result, the mill institutes, like that at Barrow Bridge mentioned earlier, became increasingly like social clubs, and it became clear to even the most faithful believer in progress what sort of recreation was the most popular among the working-class. Although the effect on popular leisure of self-improvement facilities provided at mills was strictly limited, the factory community none the less acted as an important social centre. 'Much of what was an integral part of daily life' (writes Patrick Joyce), '— a smoke, the reading of a newspaper, playing in a brass band — . . . took place within the territory of the factory'. In Bolton, the importance of the employer in providing new recreations from the 1850s, both in the factory and in the town, became everywhere apparent.[14]

The 1850s saw the first municipal provision for leisure in Bolton in the form of the public library. Opened in 1853, this was very popular, for it drew upon the large and lively reading public which Bolton already possessed. Commercial literature had long been popular. As early as 1814, Bolton had six booksellers (more than today) and in 1824 there were three circulating libraries, two of them run by booksellers; and this was even before the 1830s boom in cheap penny publications. The monthly subscription to a commercial library was about 1/3, and a typical catalogue would be 'stocked almost entirely with hack-work' — what were later known as 'penny dreadfuls'. Such publications attracted a 'serious if naive' readership of (it was alleged) 'shop-boys, vacant-minded "gents" and sentimental misses', most of whom would have learned to read at Sunday schools.

Reformers were sometimes disturbed that the precious gift of literacy was used to indulge existing 'debased' tastes for stories of murders, monsters and melodrama. The Wesleyan Methodists thus had their own circulating library from the early nineteenth century, and although well-used, it was criticised for being 'too sectarian in tone'; all fiction and plays (including Shakespeare) were excluded as likely to 'weaken and deprave' the mind. [15]

Bolton's free public library, although 'improving' in overall intent, was much more democratic in tone. It was financed partly through a rate under the new Public Libraries Act and partly by a local appeal. A special 'Working Men's Committee', set up to raise money from the working class, met, however, with a disappointing level of apathy and even hostility from people who felt they would not use the new library because they already had access to books or lived too far away, or who could not read, or who had been disappointed by the failure of earlier appeals for the Athenaeum and a park. The new library was non-sectarian and stocked plenty of popular fiction (though not 'trash'). The hopes for its effects were more modest than they might have been had it been founded a generation earlier:

> We do not expect that this library [said the ex-mayor in his opening speech] is all at once, and suddenly, to turn a man's habits from being of a degraded and sensual nature to being of an educated and intellectual character; though this we believe will be the tendency and may in time to a considerable extent be effected . . . At all events, should this library do no more than afford innocent amusement and recreations to numbers of our artisans and operatives at their own firesides during the ensuing winter, instead of spending their evenings at the alehouse or the public streets, to the neglect of their families . . . our labour has not been in vain. [16]

(A correspondent mischievously added that the following cold collation had been 'a finale of drunken revelry' with 'several cases fit for the magistrates' court'). Nearly 4,000 people joined during the first year — many 'from curiosity only' — and by 1867 there were some twelve-and-a-half thousand on the roll. 11,000 of these were male, including 5,000 'artisans and labourers', 1,600 cotton workers, 1,500 juveniles, 900 clerks and book-keepers, 600 shop assistants, 350 warehousemen and 447 'persons of superior position'. 400 of the 1,372 female members were also 'persons of superior position' while the rest were dressmakers, shop assistants, schoolgirls or house-keepers. Only 32 were millhands; many probably considered themselves enrolled through their husbands, but being a working wife can have left little time for reading.

A free library was a novel boon, and the books were treated very carefully. Remarkably few were lost or damaged, and men who came straight from work in oily clothes would bring napkins to wrap their books. There was a self-improving, status-conscious artisan élite using the library. One deputation of working men complained to the librarian that 'the books in the lending library were not of a sufficiently high character for them' and asked to be allowed to borrow books from the reference library, for they 'did not choose to sit in the same room with the men and boys who work under them, but would rather read their books at home'. The overwhelming demand, however, was for fiction and 'general literature' (mainly magazines), which accounted for up to five out of every six loans. In 1854, the librarian reported that there had been:

> Many applications for new and popular works such as *Bleak House* or *The Lamplighter*. Six copies of the latter book were presented a month ago, and such would be the case for some time were the number of copies increased to fifty . . .

The high-minded pioneers of the public library accepted the inevitable with good grace, but the stern character of the library did not change, and over the years, 'library attendents became minor ogres in working-class folklore'. Alice Foley recalled her weekly visits to the library in the early 1900s:

> I usually crept upstairs to the reading room, trying to still the patter of my clogs on the stone steps, but on settling down with a picture magazine, up came an irate caretaker, and I was shunted out like an unwanted animal.

She would then bring home the books she had borrowed, and silence descended on the household as her family started reading.[17]

The post-1850 consensus in Bolton that 'intellectual improvement' for the working-class was a good thing brought with it agreement that this alone was not enough; 'physical improvement' was important too. 'No man', it was felt, 'could have his mental, social or religious energies brought properly into play if his physical powers were jaded or debased'. Besides, physical recreation would tend 'to civilise the working classes and keep them away from the beerhouse'. There was said to be 'scarcely a town in the kingdom so destitute of open spaces as Bolton'.[18] A park, however, was much more expensive than a library, and early developments depended, not always successfully, on private initiatives. The first attempt to provide Bolton with a park floundered on the old political divisions. In 1850, the Liberal Robert Heywood led a scheme to establish a Peel Park in Bolton, named after the late Sir Robert Peel, the former Conservative Prime Minister. It was hoped that the choice of name would make it acceptable to all parties, but in fact both Tories and radicals saw the park as a bluff staged by the other in order that it would fail and bring discredit on their opponents. Poor Heywood was left trying to pacify both sides, and the plan floundered on further complications over the size of the government grant, the price of land and Sunday opening. Its failure left a bitter taste for years to come.[19] Soon after, Lord Bradford, a Tory landowner who had boycotted the Peel Park scheme, stepped in to offer a small plot of land as an alternative park, named after himself. Its opening in 1854 was accompanied by an almost embarrassing lack of interest. The *Bowtun Loominary* derided the gift, claiming that it yielded the Lord, 'a pretty big annual income': 'Aw wunder uz th'Bowtuners durnt nail a protest ogen its beein cawd a perk to th'durpost oth main entrance', wrote the editor.[20] The following year, Robert Heywood himself offered some land for a public park, on condition two other plots could be found for the same purpose. They could not, and the plan floundered, damaged also by opposition from respectable residents near the proposed site who feared a working class invasion of their quiet neighbourhood.

It took the poverty of the cotton famine of 1862–5 to bring about any further municipal provision for recreation in Bolton. There was undoubtedly fear that working-class distress would bring political insurrection similar to that of the 1830s and 1840s, and there were various moves to provide ways of giving the unemployed something pleasant and harmless to do with their time. The Mechanics' Institute opened its newspaper room free during this period, and a working men's club was founded (see below), but the first and biggest project was for a public park, the building of which also provided work for some of the unemployed between 1862 and 1865. The public park in Bolton was actually preceded by that at Farnworth, which was donated by the local manufacturer Thomas Barnes and opened in 1864. Bolton Park (later Queen's Park) was, after the Town Hall, the biggest municipal project of its time, and cost an unprecedented £57,000. The park, and the Heywood Recreation Ground next door, were opened by Gladstone in 1866, amid the now-familiar predictions of the working-class 'improvement' which would follow from the provision of grass, flowers, seats, bowling greens and 'gymnastic equipment' (as the childrens' climbing frames were referred to).[21] These last could not be used on Sundays, and soon a controversy arose over whether the park should be open on the Sabbath. The Sabbatarians argued that such a move would draw people from church and sap the moral fibre of the town, but the *Bolton Chronicle* disagreed:

> Let the park be opened. It will attract the vicious and ignorant, and make them less vicious and ignorant. It will not withdraw one conscientious observer from either church or chapel. It will open up rural delights and pleasures which can never be hurtful . . . is it not better than drinking in a crowded court? The men who rise from tippling to Park-walking will bring up sons who will rise from park-walking to religious worship.[22]

The council agreed (just) and the park was opened, but another fierce wave of Sabbatarian opposition had to be fended off in 1869 before the Park's Sunday visitors could buy refreshments. Even so, the bye-laws still kept the children from their climbing frames on the Sabbath, while Sunday brass band music was not permitted until the present century.[23] None the less, the park was a popular Sunday resort, even though the relative cheapness of the site had placed it downwind of the town's industries, near the polluted Croal and right over a 'foul and objectionable stream' which an ornamental bridge could do little to improve.[24]

During the remainder of the century, Bolton acquired several parks of different sizes from private donors. Much the most notable was the huge Mere Hall estate, library and museum, donated in a remarkable act of generosity by the manufacturer J. P. Thomasson and opened in 1890. These developments, however, did not bring about the transformation of manners that their promoters envisaged, any more than they could alter the overwhelmingly brick-and-stone environment of a great city which continued expanding for generations more. At the end of the nineteenth century Bolton Park appeared from a distance as 'an island of dingy green in a sea of black'.[25]

The other important leisure development of the cotton famine in Bolton was the Bank House working men's club. This was established in 1863–4, following national initiatives, by Bolton gentlemen of all political colours, with active support from many workers. The object was 'to provide instruction, recreation and social improvement for the working-classes, free from sectarianism and party politics'. Bank House, a converted private residence, contained meeting rooms for clubs and societies, to keep them away from the pubs (and, perhaps, from the subversive underground with which pubs may still have been associated in the middle-class imagination). There were also newspapers, books and board games, and some popular lectures. The club attracted more than 500 visits a week, by no means all of them from people who sought improving and 'rational' recreation. The ban on alcohol caused disputes in the management. Uncomfortable facilities, insistence that the club be self-financing, and a lack of bar profits to make it so, caused the club to fold in 1869. A fresh start was made in the 1870s, and, following the triumph of the popular, beer-drinking faction in the national Club and Institute Union in 1884, working men's clubs spread and prospered as places of straightforward enjoyment.[26]

The decline and collapse of the Bank House club coincided with the early spread in Bolton of Conservative working-men's clubs, rather as the failure of the élite Town Club project around the same time was followed by the establishment of a Conservative Club for the upper and middle classes. These clubs were the indirect descendents of the Operative Conservative Associations of the 1830s, which had been more concerned with organising election mobs than with leisure or improvement.[27] There were 31 Conservative working men's clubs in Bolton by 1887, with nearly 3,000 members in all. The whole operation provided social cement for the Conservative hegemony in the town, following upon the Conservative seizure of control on the town council in 1869. Liberal clubs for working men followed but, judging from their fewer appearances in billiards and other competitions, they were less successful. However, the fact that the rival organisations came together in leisure shows that the difference between them was much less than that between temperance/radical and bacchanalian/Tory cultures of fifty years before.[28]

Brass band music also developed rapidly in this period, and numerous successful bands were formed in association with factories, churches and temperance societies.[29] Brass bands were expensive to begin, and needed this sort of patronage, but having gained it, many went on to become independent of their founders with remarkably little fuss. This tolerant patronage was partly because music was regarded as 'the most incorruptible of the arts'; partly because there was already a tradition in Bolton of respectable working-class interest in music; and partly because there was a tradition of disreputable working-class interest in music, through the pubs, singing rooms, and noisy drum and fife bands, to which proper brass bands were doubtless seen as an alternative. Both these traditions also contributed to the popularity of the brass band movement from the working-class point of view.

The drum and fife band was an earlier and poorer relation of the brass band. Its original connection was with morris dancing and rush-bearing customs. Its later connection was with the noise and racket of urban streets, particularly at holiday times, when the authorities would 'not usually interfere'. Some of these bands were simply impromptu gatherings of resourceful drunks. Others were more formally constituted, such as the Teetotal Drum and Fife Band — 'an unruly mob', according to one sleepless resident near the Temperance Hall.[30] The first formally organised band in Bolton was Bolton Old Band, formed in the late eighteenth century and run for many years by the notorious local magistrate, Colonel Fletcher — William Cobbet's 'Bolton Fletcher'. It contained a colourful cross-section of players from all classes — a mill manager, farmers, several innkeepers (including Thomas Sharples of the Star Concert Room), cotton workers, hand-loom weavers, a collier and an Irish painter. Some of them were ruined by drink; most were highly dedicated, 'decent, and well-conducted'. The serpent player was a strict sabbatarian: when he failed to arrive home from one concert until after dawn broke on a Sunday, he buried his instrument for good (though he dug it up later to sell it). Cotton mills produced the earliest modern brass bands. Eagley Mills had one as early as 1837, while the band at Thomas Barnes's, Farnworth, was begun by a gift of £120 from the owner, and was taught by his son. Classical music became very popular in Bolton, as in other Lancashire industrial towns, and any classical concerts which were effectively open to the working class were rapidly sold out.[31] By the time the Volunteer force was formed in 1859, they needed to look no further than St. Peter's Church for an official band; when St. Peter's held out for money, they were replaced by 'a ruck o'knobsticks from the country' in the shape of Farnworth Old Band, who undercut them.[32] Farnworth Old Band was formerly Barnes's Band; like so many others, it went independent once it was established. Nearly all the successful local bands of the 1930s had started out attached to some institution in the previous century. As well as the institutional bands, there were also some family bands, such as the remarkable Bleackley Family Orchestra. This was the product of a lifetime's dedication by James Bleackley, an orphan who had begun his working life at the age of ten in a factory. Years of hard work, thrift and procreation, combined with a strict family regime of enforced musical practice, made him by the 1890s the leader of a popular orchestra consisting of himself and nine offspring.[33]

Perhaps the most successful leisure development of the mid-Victorian period in Bolton was the railway excursion. At the centre of the world's earliest railway network, Boltoners soon took advantage of their position to make trips to the seaside. One of the earliest railway excursions in the country left Farnworth for Liverpool — then a fashionable resort — in 1836. The organiser was a firm now familiar to us through the sponsorship of a brass band and a park, Thomas Barnes and Son of Farnworth. Barnes negotiated a reduced fare of 4/- return for 300 workers with the Bolton and Kenyon Railway Company. This was in fact a direct continuation of the established custom of sea bathing, which was particularly strong in the Bolton area. A Birmingham lady noticed at Blackpool in 1788: 'A species called Boltoners . . . rich, rough, honest manufacturers of the town of

Bolton whose coarseness of manner is proverbial even among own countrymen'. In 1811 Bolton's ordinary people, as they had done for many years past, clubbed together for an annual trip to the sea at Liverpool, where people of all ages and both sexes would bathe naked together.[34]

Reformers saw in railway excursions an opportunity to promote recreation which was wholesome, relaxing, invigorating and suitable for all the family — everything, in short, which recreations should be, and free of the wasteful and disreputable temptations of the pub and the street. Trips were organised not only by the railway companies but by mills, churches and Sunday schools. They were seen as up-to-date extensions of the usual tea-parties and celebrations, and (by the Sunday schools) as a good way of keeping children from local fairs and wakes. However, excursions succeeded because they accorded well with what people already enjoyed. A day trip was a supplement to, not a replacement for, a three-day wakes or fair. In fact, the railway helped wakes and fairs by shipping in crowds from a much wider area than before. It was also put to other popular uses which did not meet with respectable approval. In the 1850s, when more stable economic conditions led to the first sustained growth in the popularity of excursions, there was a fashion for visiting relatives by train on Sundays, when Boltoners left 'as if there were a plague in the town', much to the disgust of Sabbatarians. The guards on the Sunday trains would also carry homing pigeons to be released from different destinations, their return flights eagerly awaited and timed by knots of sabbath-breaking pigeon fanciers.[35]

A regular cycle of cheap trips throughout the summer became established, and for rather less than ten shillings, passengers could visit as far afield as North Wales, the Lake District, the Yorkshire coast or Ireland. Two and three day holidays became more common after the cotton famine of 1862–5. By 1871, the cheap trips organised in early August by various groups of cotton operatives in Bolton had become a full-blown annual holiday, with all the mills shut for two or three days — a modern 'wakes' where none had existed before. The tradesmen's annual holiday followed soon, at a distance of a few weeks. Whitsuntide remained, however, the biggest holiday of the year (36,000 people left the town in Whit Week 1861), and Bolton was the last major Lancashire town to gain a full week's summer holiday, which it achieved in the early twentieth century.[36] Many wakes and fairs, while at first confirmed in their popularity by the coming of railway excursions, eventually dwindled as domestic occasions because of the growing rush to the seaside. Larger pleasure fairs, however, such as those at Turton, at Farnworth Wakes and at Whit and New Year in Bolton, simply grew bigger throughout the century as commercial pleasure fairs, the railways bringing huge crowds to enjoy them.

As for Christmas, Bolton was slow on the uptake as the festival caught on in the rest of Britain in the 1840s. In the 1830s, most Bolton mills closed only during divine service on Christmas Day (and some not even then) and closing for the day was still by no means universal in the 1860s. The main holiday was at the new year, and the New Year Fair was Bolton's biggest. The run of plans which survives enable us to trace the growth of ever more elaborate steam roundabouts and other

Fig. 5   Centenary rally of Bolton's Nonconformist Sunday Schools, Victoria, Square, 1880.

attractions at the fair between the 1890s and the 1920s, and the sad decline of the hot pea stall, in favour of a curious mid-winter taste for ice cream.[37]

The seaside holiday, then, was the most obviously successful of the new recreations of the Victorian age. Although welcomed by advocates of recreational reform, this success happened very much on the working-class's own terms. Popular demand, not moral desirability or reforming campaigns, decided what sort of leisure was available. It must be admitted, however, that Tory opposition in the earlier part of the century and the establishment of a Conservative hegemony in Bolton in the later part did hamper the development of a working-class culture of 'improvement' such as existed more strongly in, say, Rochdale or Manchester. The 1860s and 1870s saw a change in direction for the institutions which catered for working-class improvement. The non-alcoholic Bank House working men's club, as we have seen, collapsed, and was later replaced by something more straight-forwardly sociable. In the late 1850s, the committee of the Mechanics' Institute accepted that it was not, after all, going to improve the working-class as a whole, and decided to pursue a more self-financing policy of providing education for those who were in practice the institute's supporters. The opening of larger

30

premises was delayed until 1868 when the novelist Anthony Trollope opened an impressive new building; his pious expressions of hope for the advancement of civilisation were out of step with the institute's more limited aims. Within a few years, the membership more than doubled to over 700, thanks partly to a new billiard table. The institute completed its evolution when it was absorbed into the new technical college opened in 1897.[38] Mill institutes, as described above, tended to become more like social clubs as they sprouted games and sports facilities designed in the first place to attract more people to the serious business of self-improvement. Finally, the Sunday schools underwent a prolonged and subtle change in outlook. Originally designed to build the working class in a new image, their original strategy had been a mixture of reform (tea parties, outings and religious instruction) and repression (campaigns against Sunday leisure, pubs and music halls). The failure of this duel strategy to produce any obvious changes in society produced after 1870 a philosophy that anything which could attract children away from sin was worth putting on for its own sake. The Sunday Schools Social League, formed in 1889 as the Bolton Lads' Club, became the town's biggest organising force for juvenile sport, as well as a superficially successful means of recruitment for the schools.[39] Originally, the Sunday schools saw themselves as the alternative society; now, they saw themselves as alternatives within society. The Sunday schools realised that their most popular service was recreation and capitalised upon it, drawing justification from the high ideals which surrounded sporting activity at the time. Their development within society, conditioned by what was popular rather than creating a new popularity, mirrored that of other institutions which provided reformed recreation for the working class. In the last third of the nineteenth century, Bolton's varied network of social institutions provided a base for the development of modern sport, which soon assumed a momentum and character all of its own.

## The Rise of Sport

Sport, in many ways, was 'the great leveller'. Both Liberals and Tories, 'improvers' and 'traditionalists' joined in its promotion. Sporting developments in Bolton, however, still reflected class divisions, particularly in the earlier stages, when promoters' ideas of what was respectable conditioned what sports were on offer. In an industrial town with almost no public open space, new ventures needed patrons who could control the allocation of land. However, the first sports to become established paved the way for others to develop, and in the space of a generation, popular sport quite outgrew its beginnings as an appendage of mid-Victorian society and took on a life of its own.

In the earlier nineteenth century, the word 'sport' conjured up images of the pastimes patronised by the upper classes — hunting, prize fighting, cockfighting and cricket. These were mostly unacceptable to middle-class reformers, who denounced 'debased' indulgences and concentrated on building their own leisure world based on education and self-discipline — decent and constructive recreations which were often described as 'rational'. Around the middle of the

Fig. 6   Bowlers on the Green at the Spread Eagle, Turton, *c*.1890. The landlord is standing, first from the right.

nineteenth century, the concept of 'rational recreation' widened to include sports and games. The slogan of 'a healthy mind in a healthy body' was often heard. Ethelbert Entwhistle, the son of a local ironfounder, put forward the ideals of 'rational recreation' in a lecture to the Bolton Parish Church Mutual Improvement Society in 1881:

> The effect of the games of our youth on after life is incalculable. Not only is our physique improved by them, but they exert also a great influence on our character; promptitude in action, courage, energy and cheerfulness, are among the pastimes cultivated by such pastimes as cricket, skating, bicycling, swimming, rowing, and many others. To these, may we not attribute, to a certain extent, England's proud position as one of the foremost nations of the earth.

The general rule for recreations was that there should 'be a system about them, so that the greatest possible good be derived from the least expenditure of time'. Entwhistle's own favourite pastime was skating and he put a lot of effort in providing ropes and lifebelts on local ponds to make the sport safer. There was, however, a sad postscript to all this; eleven days after delivering his lecture, Ethelbert Entwhistle fell through the ice at Bradford Lodge and was drowned.[40]

The Victorian code of sportsmanship drew not only upon 'rational' reforming ideas but also upon an older aristocratic outlook, concerned with sport as a way of keeping the masses happy and stiffening the national fibre (arguments which had

32

earlier been heard in defence of bull-baiting). In fact, it was sports which were already popular with the upper classes which first earned the 'rational recreation' seal of approval. Billiards, for example, was long thought of as disreputable, owing to its association, because of the expense of tables, with the idle rich and the pub. In 1840, however, Bolton acquired an exclusive billiard club, and the view took root that billiards was really a very scientific and rational pastime. By the 1870s, billiard tables were appearing in political and social clubs all over the town, and public tournaments and leagues followed.[41] A similarly high opinion emerged of bowls, another established gentlemen's recreation adopted by the middle class. Bolton had several private subscription bowling greens in the 1830s, often attached to pubs, and the West End Bowling Club, formed in 1854, became a place where the industrial and commercial élite of the area met each other.

Eagley Mill had a bowling green for its workers as early as 1837, and in the 1860s and 1870s, public greens appeared in parks, or run by limited companies. This did not, however, prevent bowls from becoming a popular pub sport, and there were the inevitable clashes of interest between those who sought to make bowls into a 'rational recreation' and those who just wanted to play it; the green at Farnworth Park was unfortunately next door to a pub, and a nearby resident complained that it was the scene of betting, swearing and 'torrents of evil'.[42] Quoits was another pub game which was taken up, but not transformed, by the apostles of 'rational recreation': Robert Heywood included space for 'coiting' in his recreation ground in 1866. The *Bowtun Loominary* gleefully satirised such progressive attitudes in a piece entitled: 'The Merch o Intelleckt, — No. 30. The Spoarts o'th'Workin' Class. — O Koytin' Match!' Quoits remained a pub game until it was generally displaced by darts in the 1930s. No similar moves were made to civilise bagatelle or dominoes, which smacked too much of gambling ever to be considered acceptable.[43]

Running was also too strongly identified with working-class pub life and betting to become quickly popular among the middle classes. Gymnastics caught on first, producing the figure of the stern Victorian strong man in moustache and leotard with which we are so familiar. The Bolton Amateur Swimming Club was formed in 1871 (and had to contend for many years with the chilly waters of the old town baths). Cycling began to catch on at around the same time. In the 1870s too there was a vogue for ice skating, either on the town's many frozen mill lodges or, for those without skates of their own, on the commercial rink which opened in 1876. Women as well as men could go skating, and improvements in bicycle design and the invention of the pneumatic tyre made cycling very popular among young men and women. Many women also joined in the with the more middle-class sport of tennis in the 1890s — middle-class because it was played in private clubs such as that formed at Haulgh in 1896.[44] For Bolton's upper crust, the exclusive golf club at Smithills was opened in 1896. New recreational developments were often accompanied by societies which provided all sorts of reasons why they were a Good Thing, but the simple truth was that Bolton's young middle classes were finding out that, after all, there was nothing wrong with enjoying yourself.

For the working class, finding time rather than finding pastimes on which to bestow moral approval, was the biggest bar to enjoying sport. The Saturday half-holiday was imposed throughout the cotton industry in 1850, and by 1871 was 'a recognised institution' in all branches of Bolton's industry. Shop assistants had to wait longer; after repeated failed campaigns, the Wednesday half-holiday did not properly catch on in the area until 1890.[45] The first sport to be promoted on a large scale in the Bolton area as suitable for the working class was cricket. As a long-established gentlemen's sport, it had unbroken links with the Tory élite, while as a public school sport, it was early accepted by the middle class as healthy and rational. Working-class people took to cricket readily, for bat and ball games were already familiar, and it smacked little of the repressive moralism of other attempts by the middle class to keep them decently amused. Cricket's early popularity among all classes meant that it was an important pathbreaker for other less respectable sports, notably football, to be introduced by patrons in their modern forms.

There was a gentleman's cricket club in Bolton as early as 1833, and four by 1852. The game was given a big local boost by the immensely popular visits of the All-England team in the 1860s, as well as by the Saturday half-holiday, and by 1867 there were over 70 teams in the Bolton area. Cricket was widely regarded as 'an innocent and manly recreation' and 'a civilising influence in the towns', and many of these clubs were attached to mills (to Eagley Mill in the 1830s) and churches. Middle-class players saw fair play and the amateur spirit as the most important part of the game, but working-class teams saw nothing wrong in paying good players in order to keep them, or in a little betting on the side. One gentleman who had just scored 70 for a local team modestly but unwisely refused a collection made for him, and the collector:

> wrongly judged it to be a touch of snobbery and in a caustic manner, he handed the money to a club official, declaring with asperity, "Here, tak' it. He wants no money, maulin' abeht wi' a collar an' tie aw wik".

Gentlemen's teams, however, also employed the odd resident professional; the almost mythical figure of the fast bowling blacksmith was a reality in Bolton. The amateur/professional distinction made the game a microcosm of class society, where Bolton Cricket Club's professional bowled in clogs 'as if to acknowledge his status'. The Club helped other sports to get off the ground, and its grounds came to accommodate bowls, rugby union, football and lacrosse. Cricket clubs, along with brass bands and, later, football clubs, were among the leading organisers of the fund-raising athletics festivals which became popular summer events during the 1860s. Many football clubs grew out of cricket clubs who wanted to find a use for their grounds in the winter.[46]

After over fifty years during which football was regarded as 'a boys' game', fit only to be played in the street, modern football developed in the 1870s. It was helped greatly by the spread of the Saturday half-holiday among factory workers. The first club in the Bolton area was Turton, and its progress neatly illustrates the

34

game's development. Turton FC was founded in 1871 by two sons of James Kay of Turton Tower, who had learnt to play football at Harrow public school. The village schoolmaster helped to run the club, which was seen as part of a general move towards improving the working-class, for it was at first only for members of the local reading room and institute. The team was successful and, like many other local clubs, began to pay its players with some of the money it was earning from spectators. It helped to found the Lancashire Football Association in 1878, but this was at first an amateur body, so the club campaigned for the rules to be changed to allow players to be paid. Bolton Wanderers had a similar history; they were formed in 1872 as Christchurch Football Club, but threw off their original church patrons, and campaigned for professionalism to be allowed in the national F.A. Working men, it was claimed, 'cannot play the game on strictly amateur lines . . . They cannot afford to train, or to "get in form".' The battle for professionalism was eventually won, and football became a commercial spectator sport. This was to the advantage of a big town club like the Wanderers, but not in the end to the advantage of a small out-of-town club like Turton; after paving the way for modern football, Turton ended up in the Lancashire Combination while Bolton Wanderers went on to help found the professional Football League in 1889.

Football rapidly became a way of letting off aggression in local partisanship — supporting the Wanderers, as one fan put it, 'reminded you that you were a Bolton lad and not one of them Bury lot'. If a bad result was thought to be the referee's fault, the pitch would be bombarded with sticks and orange peel, and officials and players might even be assaulted as they left the field. Women were no strangers to the passions of football, as the unpopular referee of the Great Lever vs. Preston cup tie in 1884 found:

> After the affair was over I was attacked by a mob of infuriated beings in petticoats, supposed to be women, who were without doubt in some cases mothers, if I may judge from the innocent looking babes suckling at their breasts. They brandished their umbrellas and shook their fists in my face.

A big match was a major local event. At an 1884 cup tie with Notts. County, the Wanderers ground overflowed and some 4,500 people paid local farmers half the normal entry price to watch from their fields. On the day of another Bolton vs. Notts. County cup tie in 1908, one local firm found that 22 of its workers turned up while 329 stayed away to watch the match.

Middle-class people attended football matches in substantial numbers in the late nineteenth century, sometimes with their wives and lady friends. They tended to applaud the ideals of good sportsmanship and keen amateurism, and increasingly came to regard the commercial game as a 'moral slough'. Gamesmanship, bad crowd behaviour and the 'fashionable brutality' of the professional foul were blamed on the corrupting lure of money. Such criticism was hopeless. By 1880 there were already some seventy teams in the Bolton area, and although many of them had begun life attached to churches, mills and institutes, a lot of money was clandestinely circulating to players, and the popularity of football meant that

Fig. 7   Bolton Temperance Football Club, 1903. This was an amateur club, but many professional clubs, including the Wanderers, also started life connected to churches, mills, temperance societies and other 'improving' organisations.

commercialism and competitiveness were already built into the game. In the 1890s, however, once the professional game became well-established, there was a fresh wave of amateur clubs formed, particularly after the advent of the Wednesday half-holiday for shops in 1890. The Bolton and District Amateur Football League was formed in 1890 and the Bolton Wednesday League in 1900, with such clubs as Bolton Co-op, Bolton Post Office Recreation Club, Bolton Pawn-Brokers' Assistants and Bolton Wednesday. Organised schools' football also got underway in the 1890s. Within twenty-five years modern football in Bolton had progressed from its very beginnings into the present two-tier amateur and professional system, becoming the most popular of all mass spectator sports.[47]

The story of popular leisure in the nineteenth century has in the past been seen in terms of a sad decline of rural pastimes, followed (especially in the growing towns) by a 'leisure vacuum' in the 1820s to 1840s, and then a slow but sure growth of modern recreations through the efforts of various patrons, reformers and organisers. This study has tried to avoid such a narrative, and to show how popular demand often determined the success and direction of recreational reforms. Even so, a generalised view of progress is inevitable unless the developments are set in perspective against the much more slowly-changing background of popular social life. The most important part of this, as it had been before the industrial revolution and as it still is today, was the pub.

*Notes*
1. *Bolton Bee*, No. 1 (June 1851); Bailey, *Leisure and Class in Victorian England*, Chapter 3.
2. Rhodes Boyson, *The Ashworth Cotton Enterprise* (Oxford, 1970), Chapters 6 and 7; Leon Faucher, *Manchester in 1844* (1844; reprinted London, 1969); A. B. Reach, *Manchester and the Textile Districts in 1849*, ed. C. Aspin (Helmshore, 1972), pp. 65–70; William Dodd, *The Factory System Illustrated* (1842; repr. London, 1968), pp. 62–71; Select Committee on the Operation of the Factory Acts, *Parliamentary Papers* 1840, x, pp. 1–24, 37–60.
3. J. S. Marsden and D. B. S. Brock, 'Eagley Mills, 1800–1965' (unpublished typescript in *BRL*); 'An Account of Eagley Mills, 1860' (taken from *BC* 10.11.1860, pamphlet in *BRL*).
4. D. O'Connor, 'Barrow Bridge' typescript, pp. 61–74, 83–6, 104–10, 129–39; *idem.*, *Barrow Bridge* (Bolton, 1972); C. Aspin, *Lancashire, The First Industrial Society* (Helmshore, 1969), p. 137; *BC* 26.10.1872.
5. *BC* 27.5.1843; 20.1.1872.
6. *History of Bolton Sunday Schools* (Bolton, 1880); J. Black, *op. cit.*, pp. 70–1. On drink: Harwood Wesleyan Methodist Temperance Society Minutes Book (*BRL*: NMWW/10, 3/1); Park Street Wesleyan Sunday School Record Book (*BRL*: NMWP/2, 2/8); Bridge Street Wesleyan Church Circuit Book (*BRL*: NMWB/1, 7/1); James Johnston, *Mawdsley Street Chapel* (London, 1908), p. 127; Cottrell, *Gate Pike*, Chapter 7.
7. R. D. Storch, 'The Problem of Working-Class Leisure', in A. P. Donajgrodski (ed.), *Social Control in Nineteenth Century England* (London, 1977), pp. 150–1.
8. *BC* 12.9.1829; *BFP* 30.9.1837; Select Committee on Public Libraries, *Parliamentary Papers* 1849, xi, p. xvii, Appendix 3; for controversy, see *BC* 14–21.8.1830; 29.8–3.10.1829; Mechanics' Institute Annual Report, 1841 (in Heywood Papers, *BRL*, ZHE/37/10); Mabel Tylecote, *The Mechanics' Institutes of Lancashire and Yorkshire Before 1851* (Manchester, 1957).
9. Trygve R. Tholfsen, *Working-Class Radicalism in Mid-Victorian England* (London, 1976), pp. 107–9; *English Chartist Circular* vol. II, no. 110 (copy in *BRL*).
10. *BC* 14.11.1846.
11. Heywood Papers, ZHE/42/45–50; *BFP* 12.12.1846, 5.7.1851.
12. *BC* 12–26.8.1865, 29.10.1870.
13. *BC* 18.11.1854; Joyce, *op. cit.*, pp. 144–5 and Chapter 4.
14. Joyce, *op. cit.*, p. 172.
15. Select Committee on Public Houses, *Parliamentary Papers* 1854, p. xiv: evidence of J. Cunliffe, Bolton Temperance campaigner, p. Q2388–9; Louis James, *Fiction for the Working Man* (1963; rep. Penguin, 1973), Chapter 1; *BC* 12.9.1829, 25.11.1854, 12.12.1859; Tom Dunne, 'A History of Public Libraries in Bolton, from the Beginnings to 1974' (University of Strathclyde, Ph.D. thesis, 1981).
16. Borough of Bolton Public Library and Museum: Proceedings of the Working Men's Committee (*BRL*: MS 517/8); *BC* 15.10.1853; Bailey, *op. cit.*, p. 50, wrongly gives the opening date as 1852.
17. Bolton Public Library Annual Reports, 1854, 1866, 1867; Dunne, thesis; Bailey, *op. cit.*, p. 84; Alice Foley, *A Bolton Childhood* (Manchester, 1973), pp. 24–5.
18. M. H. Elsworth, 'The Provision for Physical Recreation in Bolton in the Nineteenth Century' (Dip.Ed. dissertation, University of Manchester, 1972, pp. 7–22); Heywood Papers ZHE 47/7; *BC* 22.7.1850, 31.10.1857.
19. Heywood Papers ZHE 46/30, 47/15, 47/40 and 47/44; *BC* 1.5.1852; Bailey, *op. cit.*, pp. 52–3.
20. *BC* 28.1.1854, 18.2.1854; *LL* 15.10.1864.
21. W. E. Brown, *Robert Heywood of Bolton* (Wakefield, 1970), pp. 60–2; Heywood Papers, ZHE/88/6; *BC* 15.6.1864–10.8.1864. (A file of these cuttings is conveniently placed in the Heywood Papers.)
22. *BC* 6.7.1867, 13.7.1867; Bolton Park Bye-Laws.
23. *BC* 13.3.1869, 17.4.1869, 15.5.1869.
24. *BC* 18.6.1864, 26.5.1866, 31.8.1872, 9.11.1872.
25. Allen Clarke, *Effects of the Factory System* (London, 1899), p. 30.
26. Greenhalgh MSS.; *BC* 31.10.1863, 7.11.1863, 5.3.1864, 29.4.1865, 3.8.1867, 24.4.1867, 24.4.1869; *LL* 2.9.1864, 9.9.1864; Cobden Club Minute Book (*BRL*); Bailey, *op. cit.*, Chapter 5.
27. W. E. Brown, *op. cit.*, pp. 27–8; Horwich Operative Conservative Association First Annual Report (*BRL*).
28. G. Evans, dissertation, pp. 22–4.
29. Series on brass bands, *BJG* 28.9.1934–22.2.1935.
30. *BC* 12.10.1850, 13.9.1851, 11.6.1859.

31. William Millington, *Sketches of Local Musicians and Musical Societies* (Pendlebury, 1884); *BC* 21.1.1854.
32. *BL* 2.6.1860.
33. *Bolton Review* (1897), pp. 275–6.
34. Alan Delgado, *The Annual Outing* (London, 1977); *BC* 7.11.1924; Harold Perkin, 'The Social Tone of the Victorian Seaside Resort in the North-West', *Northern History XI* (1976 for 1975), p. 183.
35. Ringley Wesleyan Sunday School Minutes (*BRL*), 1866 onwards, e.g. 21.4.1868; *BC* 7.9.1850, 21.5.1852.
36. *BC* 25.7–8.8.1868, 5.8–16.9.1871, 14.6.1851, 25.5.1861, 30.5.1853, 29.5.1865, 10.6.1865; on primitive conditions on excursions, see Greenhalgh MSS. For sketches of cheap trips, see *BL*, III, pp. 175–8, 185–7, 230–1, 265–8, 281–4, 289–93; VIII, pp. 201–2, 297–8, 317–8; XIII, pp. 246–7; *LL*, I, nos. 32–4.
37. *BC* 6.1.1827, 3.1.1839, 26.12.1839, 9.1.1830, 28.12.1833, 28.12.1850, 30.12.1854, 26.12.1868.
38. Mechanics' Institute Annual Reports (*BRL*). Detailed accounts of Bolton Mechanics' Institute can be found in: Derek Williams, 'An Essay to Outline the Development of Technical Education in Bolton' (Chorley College of Education, M.Ed. Dissertation, 1976); and Dunne, thesis.
39. Elsworth, *op. cit.*, pp. 23–9, 33, 78–9; *Bolton Review* 1897, pp. 163–7; *BEN* 10.6.1890; *BC* 14.6.1890.
40. Ethelbert Entwhistle, *Pastimes and Recreations* (Bolton, 1881).
41. J. H. Ainsworth, Diary (*BRL*), 10.1.1842, 6.6.1824; Bolton Billiards' Club Rules etc. (1847, *BRL*); *BC* 7.8.1852; Bailey, *Leisure and Class*, p. 60; Elsworth, dissertation, pp. 33–5.
42. *BC* 29.4.1865, 9.8.1865, 14.4.1873; West End Bowling Club subscription lists 1854 and 1864 (*BRL*); records of Rumworth Bowling Green Company (1879; PRO BT31/2525/13063, *BRL*); T. H. Winder, *A Life's Adventure* (London, 1921), pp. 29–35; *FJ* 12.8.1876. See also Alice Foley, *A Bolton Childhood*, and *The Pub and the People*, pp. 255–7.
43. Heywood Papers, ZHE/88/6; *BL* XIII (1861), p. 391.
44. Records of Haulgh Lawn Tennis Club, PRO BT31/3861/24349.
45. *BC* 19.8.1871, 16.9.1871, 28.9–16.11.1872, 14.6–26.7.1890, 30.8–8.11.1890; *BJG* 30.12.1904; J. K. Walton, 'The Social Development of Blackpool' (Lancaster University Ph.D., 1974), p. 279.
46. *BC* 5.10.1833, 10.4.1852, 13.10.1866, July–August 1867, 17.10.1868, 12.10.1872; *Bolton Cricket Club — 100 Years at Green Lane* (*BRL*); Elsworth, dissertation, pp. 27–9, 42–51, and appendices; Bailey, *op. cit.*, pp. 17, 20, 78, 128, 137, 144–5; R. G. Barlow, *Forty Seasons of First Class Cricket* (Manchester, n.d.), pp. 1–2.
47. Tony Mason, *Association Football in English Society 1863–1815* (Brighton, 1980), includes substantial material on Bolton, e.g. pp. 25, 151–3, 161, 163, 167n3, 169n39, 191, 235, 239; J. Walvin, *The People's Game* (Hamondsworth, 1975), pp. 81, 143–4; Bailey, *op. cit.*, pp. 141–4; Elsworth, dissertation, pp. 51–68 and appendices; P. M. Young, *Bolton Wanderers* (London, n.d.), Chapter 1; D. J. Hill, 'The Growth of Working-Class Sport in Lancashire 1870–1914' (Lancaster University M.A., 1975), pp. 23–6; Winder, *op. cit.*, p. 8.

# 4

# Drink and Society

Bolton's old reputation as the nonconformist 'Geneva of the North' seems to have done little to affect the taste of its upper and lower classes for drink. The pubs of early nineteenth-century Bolton were an integral part of town life. They were frequented by travellers, social groups, men on their way to work or at lunchtime, friendly societies, political groups and gentlemen visitors in coaches. The magistrates met in the higher-class pubs, and sought to control the political life of the town's working-class through their control of licensing the pubs where they met. Even the vicar, the eccentric Parsons Folds, was a great drinker, and would travel to Liverpool docks personally to pick up his Jamaica rum, sitting astride the barrel as it was carted into Bolton. To get drunk was 'the shortest way out of Manchester', and so too out of Bolton; one local beerhouse was named 'Help Me Make It Through This World', and the sign carried a picture of a man forcing apart the two hemispheres of the globe to pass through.[1]

The first working-class organisation of the industrial age to be based in the pub was a defensive one; the friendly society. These societies were closely associated in the late eighteenth and early nineteenth century with the early trade union movement, and Bolton's magistrates tried to root them out. They survived by limiting their activities to running funds for sickness and unemployment, and their regular meetings for payments were useful social occasions. By 1829 there were seventeen friendly societies in Bolton, all of them meeting in pubs; by 1850 there were over 200 lodges of various societies. They were the largest organised working-class presence in the town, and their annual meetings and dinners, and their outings and parades at Whitsun and other times, became a permanent feature of Bolton's leisure life. Despite the founding of temperance friendly societies, and of institutions such as the Working Men's Club which encouraged men to meet away from pubs, the friendly societies remained, as Mass Observation found in the 1930s, inextricably bound up with pub society.[2]

From the beginning of the nineteenth century, Saturday night was the great night of the week for leisure. People got paid, they did their week's shopping, and they went to the pub; wages were sometimes paid in large coin, which ensured they went to the pub first to change them, and have a quick drink, and then another, then another . . . publicans and employers were sometimes in league over this. There were no effective controls over drinking by children and young people, and those who worked in factories had enough money and independence to drink like their adult workmates. On New Year's Eve 1829 a *Bolton Chronicle* reporter 'observed many groups of boys in a state of intoxication' and commented:

> This is one of the bad effects of our factory system. Confined as they are, when they are let loose they run into excess.

The limited local constabulary found it quite impossible to control the late opening of pubs, shops and market stalls, and contented themselves with sorting out (where they could) some of the more violent incidents. The voluntary 'watch and ward' men in fact quit in 1820 because they had no power to enter pubs. Drunkenness amongst the constables themselves was a problem, not helped by the fact that the penalty for being drunk at the weekly meeting was a shilling in the beer kitty. The new borough force formed in 1839 was certainly no better; many were recruited from labourers and artisans who, as the reports and disciplinary records show, shared the tastes and vices of those they were supposed to discipline. Assaults on the police were commonplace, while Newtown, the Irish quarter, was virtually a no-go area for the new force. One Bolton publican drove the inspector, two constables and two magistrates out of his house with a poker. If the borough police forces, were, as has been suggested, 'the cutting edge' of bourgeois values, they were a very blunt one.[3]

Alarm at the scale of drunkenness in the industrial parts of the country was initially directed mainly against the rising consumption of spirits rather than the more traditional and ordinary drink of beer; accordingly, the 1830 Beer Act tried to break this link by allowing anyone who paid £2 for a license to set up a house selling beer only. Within ten years, Bolton had nearly 200 of these beerhouses, over which the magistrates had little control, and which were blamed for allowing betting, Sunday drinking, juvenile drinking (one was called 'Youth's Tavern'), crime and prostitution. They also provided cover for illegal cockfighting — 'the upper classes used to encourage it at one time, now the beerhouses do'.[4] In turn, the beerhouses probably aggravated the problem of illegal stills as they sought to get round the restrictions of their licences. Stills could make up to 100 gallons of potent spirit at a time, and the Irish area (as in other Lancashire towns) was notorious for illicit distilling, which was also 'carried on to an almost incredible extent' on the moors. When the tunnel for the Bolton–Blackburn line was dug under the moors, the navvies put a still at the bottom of every vertical shaft which was sunk; two excise officers in disguise, who thought they had tricked their way into inspecting the workings as they found themselves lowered down on a wooden platform, were 'accidentally' dropped into a muddy puddle at the bottom. They went home, and did not return. Much of the illegal spirit in Bolton was drunk in 'hush shops' which didn't even have a beer licence; these often traded quite blatantly, and opened at all hours, but it was almost impossible to collect evidence to prosecute them.[5] When an act of 1848 forced licensed victuallers to close for the whole of Sunday morning, rather than simply during divine service, the effect was only to drive drinkers into the hush shops; a much-resented ban on the 'gambling' game of dominoes in Farnworth pubs a few years later had a similar effect.[6]

Everyone concerned with controlling the drink trade in Bolton seems to have been keen to play down the extent of illegal drinking and to blame the beerhouse for vice, rather than the hush shops or licensed victuallers' houses: the police, because illegal drinking reflected badly on their efficiency and they preferred to blame the licensing laws; the temperance campaigners, because they did not like to admit that controls simply pushed the problems underground; and the magistrates, some of whom owned fully licensed houses whose good names they sought to preserve, and which they wanted to protect from the competition which would result from beerhouses being given full licences.[7] From the mid-1840s to the mid-1870s the number of licensed victuallers' houses in Bolton remained almost static at 118, and then rose to 127, where it remained for the rest of the century. When the 1869 Selwyn-Ibbotson bill became law and gave magistrates power to restrict beerhouse licences, the number of beerhouses fell from a peak of 329, declining to 229 by 1900. The same act, however, brought into being a number of shops and beerhouses with different varieties of wine licence and off-licence.

The growing population of Bolton, coupled with the static number of licensed houses from about 1845, meant that the profits to be gained from developing the advantages which licensed houses enjoyed over the generally humbler beerhouses, became greater. 'Dram shops', selling only spirits, sprang up as did huge gin palaces, 'selling exclusively spirits, without any room to sit down', of which there were over a dozen in 1853. Singing rooms and musical entertainments were put on in many pubs (see next chapter), and some beerhouses followed suit.[8] The importance of the city centre was further increased by the growth of new suburbs where the inhabitants had to make do with the pubs that were there when they were just villages, and after 1869, with precious few beerhouses either. In these new areas, off-licences were more common than pubs, and nearly every pub had a music or games license. In the old borough, in a period of reaction following the hotly-contested re-opening of the controversial Star Music Hall, entertainment licenses were drastically reduced in the later 1850s and early 1860s, although how much effect this had on the amount of singing, dancing and billiards-playing in pubs may be doubted. In 1872, the new Improvement Act gave the magistrates new powers over the licensing of entertainments in the town and, after an initial squeeze, this policy was reversed. The police's figures were shuffled round at this time, and give the impression that the number of 'disorderly houses', harbouring thieves, vagrants and prostitutes, was eliminated, but common sense and the local press suggest otherwise. National beer consumption and the number of arrests for drunkenness in Bolton both reached a peak in the boom of the mid-1870s.

What we may be seeing in the 1870s is an official toleration and legitimation of public house life on its own terms. As long ago as 1837, James Black, a Bolton doctor, had noticed:

> The manners, peace and outward order of the working part of society, are yearly improving. . . . Outward vice and licentiousness, as they disappear from the surface of public society, assume a less offensive garb in the retirements of beer-shops and the musical *soirees* of our tap-rooms, taverns and gin-palaces . . .[9]

For the practical Dr Black, this was progress of a sort; for the religious lobby, it was a frightening advance of devilment, and for decades a holy war was levied on Bolton's pubs and music halls by temperance campaigners and Sunday school teachers. Eventually, however, they lost the feeling that the new advance of civilisation was in danger of being wrecked by a rising tide of immorality (partly, perhaps, because the middle class was developing its own suburbs further away from the city centre), and came to view themselves more as lobbyists or missionaries than as besieged defenders. The increasing regulation of pub hours in line with the standard working week, and the gradual softening of violent manners as working-class society in Bolton became more mature and stable, made pubs appear less 'monstrous'. The rise of organised weekend sport and the growing effectiveness of policing contained and reduced the social undergrowth of gambling, street games, prostitution and general disorder which surrounded pub life. The growth of football and other organised sports and the increasing commercial enhancement of the pubs, theatres and music halls of the city centre combined to produce a weekly leisure pattern which fitted in with working hours in a regular cycle of work — letting off steam — rest — more work. There was still hardly more leisure for working women and housewives than there had been in 1800, apart from the annual excursion or holiday, Saturday night at the pub, and perhaps watching an odd football match. Underlying all the changes of the century, however (a century which we see largely through middle-class eyes), there was a huge, half-inert, slowly-changing but very active popular culture whose continuing existence and expansion to fill every new channel that was open to it was the greatest single fact of Bolton's social life. Fortunately, the rich surviving material on the town's theatres and music halls enables us to take a good long look at this popular culture as it appeared in one of its favourite resorts.

*Notes*
1.  J. D. Greenhalgh, *Parson Folds*, pp. 118–19; *The Diary of Captain Dewhurst* (Bolton, 1880 and 1881), p. 9; Greenhalgh MSS.
2.  M. Price, *op. cit.*, pp. 27 and 62; Bolton Magistrates' order 1788, *BRL* ZZ/130/13.2; *BC* 8.8.1829, 17.8.1850; *Pub and the People*, pp. 274–82.
3.  *BC* 3.1.1829; S. A. Freeman, 'The Bolton Borough Police Force, 1838–1956' (Manchester Polytechnic B.A. dissertation, 1978); J. C. Scholes, *History of Bolton* (Bolton, 1892), pp. 470–1; Great Bolton Constables' Books, e.g. 13.2.1809, 13.6.1827; R. D. Storch, 'The Plague of Blue Locusts: Police Reform and Popular Resistance in Northern England, 1849–57', *International Review of Social History, XX* (1975), pp. 61–90.
4.  *BRL, Notes and Queries*, I, pp. 154–5; Select Committee on Public Houses, *Parliamentary Papers* 1852–3, xxxvii, Q 6270–6281, and Appendix A, pp. 832–3.
5.  *BC* 9.3.1844; *BJG* 18.7.1954; *BC* 21.9.1850, 11.10.1851; Select Committee on Public Houses 1852–3, *loc. cit.*, Q 4419–4421.
6.  Bolton Chief Constable's Report, 1850; *BC* 31.1.1852, 21.2.1852, 30.12.1854.
7.  Bolton Chief Constable's Reports; Select Committee on Public Houses, 1852–3, *loc. cit.*, evidence of George Wolstenholme, J.P., pp. 247–59; Select Committee on Licensing of Places of Public Entertainment, *PP* 1854, xiv, evidence of John Cunliffe, pp. 126–37.
8.  Wolstenholme evidence, *loc. cit.*, Q 4340–3.
9.  J. Black, *op. cit.*, p. 68.

# 5
# Bolton's Old Theatre

Fig. 8   Circuses often visited Bolton in the earlier
nineteenth century.

In 1800, Bolton had a successful local theatre with an audience drawn from all social classes.[1] By 1850, the institution now known as the Old Theatre was almost defunct, having lost its higher-class clients and failed to compete successfully with the new popular music halls, which had developed independently from pub singing saloons. After another fifty years, the most profitable of the music halls had developed into sumptuous variety theatres, and were beginning to win back the respectable audience so long lost to the Bolton stage. The development of Bolton's popular theatre and music hall was closely bound up with battles for respectable status and profitability, two objectives which often conflicted. In the end, popular demand — 'the power of the penny' — purchased both.

Bolton's theatre, like Bolton itself, was already a social centre for county society at the start of the nineteenth century. The coaches of the local gentry could regularly be seen drawn up outside the building in Mawdsley Street — then part of an area bounded by the orchards and gardens of the well-to-do, called Acres Field. The Bolton Bible Society met at the theatre in the early nineteenth century and until the late 1830s plays enjoyed the occasional patronage of the Holcombe Hunt, the military, local Tory MPs and the gentlemanly Bolton Cricket Club.[2] London fashions were brought in as quickly as possible, but even in the early nineteenth century it was unusual for 'Quakers and Methodists' to visit the theatre, which was dominated by Tory society. The famous actor-manager Samuel Ryley visited Bolton about this time:

> The first night we opened the theatre, a facetious attorney just returned from hunting, amused himself and his friends by horse-whipping the fiddlers, for not playing Chevy Chase in jig time.

Patriotic and traditional themes were always popular. The theatre could act as a high-class fairground peepshow by advertising a play about the recent wars which included an 'authentic' scene of Napoleon's island prison and finished with 'a GRAND TRANSPARENCY OF THE DUKE OF WELLINGTON PAINTED, and GOD SAVE THE KING'. There was a play about a slave rising ('Humanity triumphant . . . Liberty to the Slaves') and another lambasting trade unionism ('TURN OUT, or, the CRAZY POLITICIAN'). 'Hob at the Well' recreated the scene of a traditional country wakes, right down to providing for audience participation in the rustic sports, while the ever popular 'Country Squire' allowed any social hostility to be dissipated through harmless laughter in which all sections of the audience could heartily join.[3]

The Bolton theatre also had in the second quarter of the century a limited following among the new middle-class, centred round a group of keen amateur actors. These included John Taylor, a lawyer and the borough coroner, who was an earnest, self-improving man and later a leading teetotal campaigner, though not without a sense of fun, as his autobiography shows. He and his friends were always keen to act with the groups of visiting professionals; these usually put up at the Rising Sun Inn in Churchgate, where they sold tickets and received visitors. But the social status of actors was then very low, and Taylor had to keep his acting debut secret from his family: 'Those who professed religion', he later recalled, 'considered the Theatre to be an abomination'. Prejudice against the theatre was widespread among the middle-classes for much of the nineteenth century; even Robert Greenhalgh's father, who was drama critic to the Liberal *Bolton Free Press*, was careful how he introduced his son to the pleasures of play-going.[4] 'The theatre originated in the drunken rites of Bacchus', explained one local writer in 1857: 'It is there where the passions are inflamed by the scenery, the dialogue, and the characters with whom they come into contact'. Critics could point to incidents such as the 'wanton outrage' committed in 1831 by 'some young men who had installed a quantity of wine into one of the boxes, and kept hissing and making use of disgusting language'. Several years earlier, 'A Constant Reader' of the *Bolton Express* had written:

> The part of the community that frequent a Theatre, do it for no purpose even the most distantly related to moral improvement . . . They are such of the wealthy as have neither occupation nor benevolence; the devotees of fashion; the most thoughtless part of the young, together with what are called young men of spirit, who want a little brisk folly as an interlude to their more vicious pursuits; loungers of all sorts; tradesmen who neglect their business; persons who in domestic relations have not the slightest notion of cultivating the highest social or intellectual interests; and old debauchees, together with the wretched class of beings, whose numbers, vices and miseries they can still be proud to augment . . . it is impossible for the stage to become good, in the Christian sense, because its character must become faithfully congenial with that of its supporters; and they consist of the most trifling, irreligious and immoral part of the community.

For its part, the newspaper complained that 'the progress of gloomy fanaticism' was ruining the theatre: 'the boxes are generally empty, with only a very thin sprinkling of auditors in the pit'.[5]

In 1828, Bolton's middle classes obtained their own entertainment venue when Little Bolton Town Hall* opened, and begun staging courses of topical lectures, lantern-slide shows, recitals, musical evenings, and exhibitions of scientific curiosities. Both instructive and amusing, but above all decent, these were designed to satisfy the requirements of 'rational recreation'. The Temperance Hall opened in 1844, putting on similar but much cheaper entertainments designed for a much wider audience, appealing to more of the theatre's potential custom (if, indeed, there was by now much overlap between the two audiences). In 1837, the *Bolton Free Press* noted:

> The taste of theatricals has considerably declined during the last ten or fifteen years . . . We would lay the blame on the 'march of exclusiveness', and that strong disinclination of the rich to be seen at any place of amusement to which the industrious class have easy access . . . Even where we have a good building, all else is in the hand-to-mouth misery of common barn-strollers.

Both the Tory *Bolton Chronicle* and the Liberal *Bolton Free Press*, however, continued to report on productions at the theatre. Losing its high-class audience meant the theatre had to go down-market; losing the revenue which a 'fashionable house' could bring in (up to £70 a night) meant that good actors could no longer be regularly engaged. To contemporaries, these two things seemed inevitably to go together; 'The theatre', thought John Taylor, 'was never intended for factory lads and girls'.[6] But the occasions upon which 'fashionable nights' under gentry patronage could be organised became fewer and fewer, and so the offerings became more and more popularist. Tried and tested old favourites came round increasingly often: 'Pizarro', 'The Vampire, or, the Warlock of the Glen', 'Tom and Jerry, or Life in London', 'Speed the Plough', 'The Gretna Blacksmith' and the notorious but evergreen burlesque, 'Bombastes Furioso'. The management

---

* Now Bolton's museum of local history.

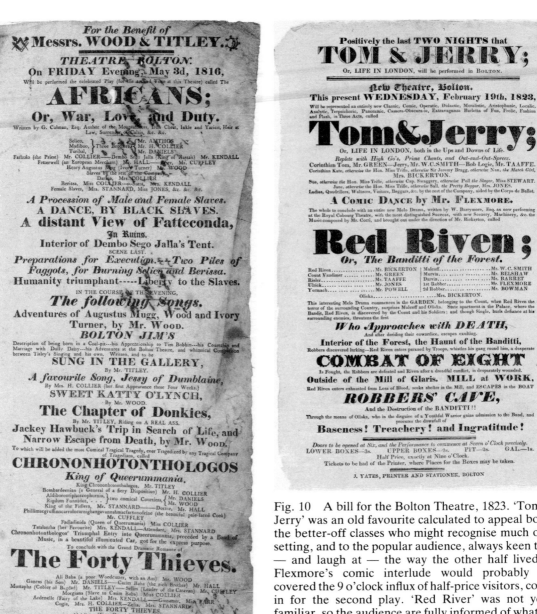

Fig. 9 A bit of everything — a night's entertainment at Bolton Theatre, 1816.

Fig. 10 A bill for the Bolton Theatre, 1823. 'Tom and Jerry' was an old favourite calculated to appeal both to the better-off classes who might recognise much of the setting, and to the popular audience, always keen to see — and laugh at — the way the other half lived. Mr Flexmore's comic interlude would probably have covered the 9 o'clock influx of half-price visitors, coming in for the second play. 'Red River' was not yet so familiar, so the audience are fully informed of what they will get for their money, even though this means giving away the entire plot.

gave the people what it wanted, and the playbills made sure the people knew they were getting it, carrying plenty of detail about plot and character (especially if the play was new to Bolton). Local themes were always popular, such as 'BOLTON JIM's Description of being born in a coal-pit . . . His apprenticeship to Tim Bobbin . . . his Courtship and Marriage with Dolly Daisy . . . His Adventures at the Bolton Theatre, and whimsical Comparison', with the song of 'Bolton is a Wonderful Town-O!' Sometimes the cast list made such detail redundant. The characters on offer in 'XYZ, or, How to Advertise for a Wife' included:

> Captain Galliard,
> Neddy Bray (a country squire),
> Old Grubbleton (an eminent solicitor),
> Roscius Alldross (an American Manager), and
> Doddle (his Factotum).

Another production offered plenty of light relief with 'Bobby Breakwindow, an unfortunate young gentleman in a jacket and corduroys', but nowhere did the cast list offer such confusion as in the play 'Chrononthotonthologos, King of Queerummania', which featured 'Bombardeenian (a general of fiery disposition)', 'Fadladinida (Queen of Queerummania)' and 'Phillimacgruffinocarrolocarnighangavannahmacfarsonofeine (the beautiful pale-faced cook)'. Plots, scenes and settings were all featured on the bills, with special attention drawn to any new scenes in well-known plays. Thus, 'The Miller and His Men' was advertised to include scenes of 'the inside of Kelmar's cottage where the robbers attempt to destroy County Friberg and his Servant Karl', 'The moveable Bridge, over which the Miller escapes' and 'Destruction of the Mill and Robbers by means of a Trail laid by Rovina to the Magazine'. No matter that this gave the plot away: the audience knew what they wanted, and wanted to be sure they were going to get it. In one production about a naval mutiny, there was a near-riot when the curtain fell just before the promised hanging, and the manager had to act fast to quell it. He quickly dressed a dummy in the condemned character's clothes:

> The curtain reascended, showing the effigy on the deck, and it was promptly jerked up to the yardarm, wriggling and twisting like a human being undergoing the tragic ordeal. The 'gods' were satisfied, testifying to their delight with loud applause, and leaving the theatre with the consciousness that they had got their money's worth out of the show.[7]

All this did not mean that the management had given up its high-class audience for lost; far from it. The £70 which a packed 'fashionable' house could bring in was well worth trying for, and managers tried to woo the town's middle class as well as the older conservative élite. The new Liberal corporation in 1839 was induced to act as patron to performances of 'The Country Squire' and Sir Lytton Bulmer's 'Lady of Lyons', starring two of the north-west's leading actors, Messrs. Brook and Neville. The following year, the manager invited the Liberal Mayor, Robert Heywood, to another evening of unsullied drama, promising that the performance would be 'totally free from local, official and political allusions'.[8] Playbills often stressed the 'good and instructive morals' of even the most lurid melodramas. 'The

47

Murdered Maid', for example, was described as 'strongly depicting the dreadful consequences of yielding to licentious passions, and the disgrace and punishments which avail such deeds', while 'The Tragedy of George Barnwell' told the 'true story' of how a convicted embezzler finally resolved 'to dedicate the rest of his life to religion and virtue'. One bill of 1823 quoted a long statement on the moral benefits of drama, recommended to 'fastidious Moralists and arrogant Philosophers'. Attempts were made to out-bid middle-class venues in offering genteel variety entertainment. The theatre's offerings in 1842 included a series of spectacular scientific entertainments 'designed to induce enquiry and elicit genius' in their audience; doses of laughing gas at 1/– a time; and the incredible 'Centrifugal Railway'. This was a mini-roller-coaster with 200 feet of track wound in a 45-foot high loop, anticipating the most modern fairground rides by 130 years. It could carry buckets of water without spilling a drop, or intrepid spectators could be whirled round it at speeds (it was alleged) of up to 100 m.p.h.[9]

The middle-class, none the less, stayed away from the theatre, whose once congenial Acres Field site was now Mawdsley Street, part of the growing and chaotic town centre. Instead, the theatre had to join in with the fierce competition for the custom of Bolton's rapidly expanding working-class. The growth of pub concert rooms and early music hall in the 1830s and 1840s coincided with a sharp drop in seat prices at the Old Theatre. In the early 1830s, the usual prices were 3/– for a box, 2/– for the pit, and 1/– for the gallery, with half-price after nine o'clock. By 1839 the pit and gallery had fallen to 1/– and 6d. respectively. By 1843, even the boxes were reduced from 3/– to 2/– 'to accommodate the nightly over-flow from the pit' — a sure sign that the high-class audience was gone — and the pit and gallery were sometimes reduced to 6d. and 3d. The old pattern of shows on Mondays, Wednesdays and Fridays ended, and performances on Saturday nights for the working-class audience were begun in 1839.[10]

The easing of licensing by the 1843 Theatres' Act brought further competition in the form of the 'Victoria Theatre' and its successors; that is semi-permanent wooden buildings put up on land in the town centre hired from the corporation. The Victoria was there for many years in the 1840s and 1850s, and up to 1,500 people at a time could be packed in (3d. for the gallery, 6d. after 9 o'clock for a box) to watch all sorts of extravagant musical productions, as well as re-enacted sea-battles and volcanic eruptions. It was also leased to private traders, and because of its famous profitability it became known (after the 1849 American gold rush) as the 'California Market'. These wooden pavilions were commonly used in this period by travelling circuses, from where the idea must have come, and this highlights the close connections between circus and theatre in the first half of the nineteenth century.[11] The established theatre, too, had long-standing links with the circus, for circus acts had regularly visited the Old Theatre in the past, and this experience was drawn on to compete with the new rival establishments. The plays offered each night became shorter and more numerous, while the intervals were filled in with jugglers, conjurers, acrobats, lion-tamers, hastily re-enacted battles and disasters with special effects, songs that were either familiar or 'stupid in the

48

extreme' (or both), spectacular chemical experiments, and even firework displays, all in an attempt to imitate the non-stop variety of the popular concert rooms. (Even so, rope dancers and illuminated views of European capitals were hopefully advertised to respectable society as 'rational amusements'.)[12]

In the end, however, the Old Theatre could not cope. It relied on working-class audiences, but it was simply not big enough to put on expensive spectacles and to pack in enough 3d. spectators to pay for them. There was not enough potential revenue to pay for good actors, and it suffered from the leasing system which gave it a succession of bad managers in the 1830s and 1840s who failed to build the sort of regular audience, style and sensitivity to popular taste which Thomas Sharples' Star Music Hall enjoyed. As a sign of the times, he bought up the Old Theatre in 1850. His son William, who had by then taken over the management of the Star from his father, used it for about 18 months after the Star burnt down in 1852, but he too seems to have been unable to make a go of it and preferred to lease it out once more. Now and again 'the élite of the borough and neighbourhood' would pack the house when a leading actor of the day was persuaded to visit, but on the whole, respectable patrons were 'literally scared away' by the low grade offerings. Even the local dialect paper, the *Bowtun Loominary*, normally a staunch defender of the people's pleasures, no longer had a good word for the Old Theatre. It was, complained the paper, a place of 'stock actors . . . more bands of stage-struck incapables . . . a lot of mere human puppets actin' plays of objectionable morality, un panderin to the lowest passions un gildin oer the worst vices of society'.[13]

In 1858, the Old Theatre was bought up by the new Bolton Concert Hall Company Ltd., established with a nominal capital of £2,500:

> to provide a Hall or Building to be used for the performance of Concerts, Oratorios, the delivery of lectures, Dramatic, and other readings, the holding of Pictorial Exhibitions, Soirees, and for other public purposes . . .[14]

(That fact that there were to be no plays, only 'dramatic readings', illustrates the extent of the prejudice against theatre.) The directors were a group of local conservative industrialists, and one printer, led ('from philanthropic motives') by the wealthy bleacher and Tory MP for Bolton, Stephen Blair. The shareholders were all local, mainly traders and industrialists (now calling themselves 'esquires'); J. T. Staton, editor of the *Bowtun Loominary*, was among the earliest. Over the next few years, the sporadic entertainments at the Old Theatre included a sparring match, a 10/6d. series of three subscription concerts, a comedy and diorama, and a lecture by a notorious tub-thumping anti-Catholic lecturer from Liverpool which was prevented from taking place by a riot staged by the considerable Irish population. The Bolton Concert Hall Company Ltd. was among the earliest attempts to use the Limited Liability Act to promote entertainment. After its disappearance in the early 1860s as an active enterprise, the site was sold for the new County Court offices, leaving Bolton's stage life in the hands of popular variety and private enterprise for the next thirty years.

*Notes*
1. The theatre was built in the late eighteenth century, as were many other provincial theatres. A cryptic entry in Winston's *Theatric Tourist* MSS. reads: '1784 Bolton-Assembly Room-Bibby-2.1 hold £30 (a theatre now here built by subscription about 4 or 5 years ago) — stayed three months'. This was written about 1803, so the theatre would have been built, or converted from an assembly room, about 1779 or 1798.
2. P. A. Whittle, *A History of Bolton Le Moors* (Bolton, 1855), p. 195; *BRL* playbills ZZ/82 1828/1, 1833/1, 1838/1; *B.Ex* 25.10.1823, 29.11.1823.
3. *BRL* playbills collection ZZ/82; S. W. Ryley, *The Itinerant, III* (London, 1808), pp. 90–6. See vol. VI (1817) for Ryley's absurd near-banishment from Bolton as a suspected revolutionary, and his assessment of the inhabitants as reactionary 'Hottentots'.
4. John Taylor, *Autobiography of a Lancashire Lawyer* (Bolton, 1883), pp. 24–39; Greenhalgh MSS.
5. *BC* 13.6.1857, 8.1.1831; *B.Ex* 18.10.1823, 25.10.1823, 15.11.1823.
6. D. O'Connor, 'Little Bolton Town Hall' (typescript in *BRL*); *BFP* 2.9.1837; Taylor, *Autobiography*, *op. cit.*, p. 33.
7. *BRL* playbills collection; Greenhalgh MSS.
8. Heywood Papers, ZHE/36/9.
9. *BRL* playbills collection, e.g. 1823/35; *BC* 22.10.1842.
10. Boxes had earlier been offered for half-price after 9 o'clock (playbill ND/28). This, however, was standard audience-pulling practice, and probably did not mean there was any lower-class invasion of the boxes.
11. Kathleen Barker, 'The People Must be Amused' in *Leisure in Britain since 1800*, edited by J. K. Walton & J. Walvin (Manchester University Press, forthcoming 1982); *BRL* playbill 1846; Greenhalgh MSS.
12. *B.Ex* 4.6.1825 (in: *BRL*, *Notes and Queries*, I, p. 138).
13. Taylor, *Autobiography*, *op. cit.*, pp. 33–5; Greenhalgh MSS; *BC* 30.11.1850; *BL* 24.6.1854. William Douglas's MSS: *Historical Account of the Provincial Theatres of England and Wales* (in New York Public Library) states that 'The principal managers of the Bolton Theatre have been, Ryley (Author of the Itinerant) 1808, Manley 1826 to 1835, W. Burroughs 1843, Corbet Cooke 1845, Preston and Weston 1846, J. Johnson 1847, Sharples 1852 to 1859, J. P. Weston 1860 to the present time' (the later 1860s).
14. *BC* 7.12.1859, 27.12.1859; Taylor, *Autobiography*, *op. cit.*, pp. 33–4; Bolton Concert Hall Company Ltd., papers, PRO BT/31/365 16534 (a copy of these has been lodged in *BRL*). The Grand Theatre in Lancaster successfully made a similar change in policy to cater for middle class tastes in 1843: see A. G. Betjemann, *The Grand Theatre, Lancaster: Two Centuries of Entertainment* (Lancaster University Centre for North-West Regional Studies, Occasional Paper No. 11, 1982), Chapter 2. According to Peter Bailey (*op. cit.*, p. 148), the first music hall in Britain to be run as a limited company was the Alhambra, Leicester Square, in 1864.

# 6
# Early Music Hall in Bolton, 1830–1855

As one of the earliest, biggest and fastest-growing of Lancashire's cotton towns, Bolton experienced, as we have seen, a rapid growth in the number of its pubs in the second quarter of the nineteenth century. This led directly to the establishment of what was arguably Britain's first music hall, the Star, in 1832. When, in the ten years after the 1830 Beer Act, nearly 200 beerhouses were set up in Bolton, many proved to be more profitable than the full licensed houses. Licensed victuallers, alarmed at this competition, began to look for ways to exploit the advantages which they held over the beerhouses. One of several consequences was the rise of the pub singing room, which rapidly evolved into the music hall. By 1853, Bolton had four or five pubs and three or four beerhouses, with special singing rooms attached, and perhaps a dozen more where there was often music; the total attendance was three or four thousand on a good night. Most of these put on simple 'free and easies' — that is, a professional musician and maybe a 'noted vocalist' would be hired, and the audience themselves would sing along, or take the stage to provide their own entertainment. Two of these, however, had large, purpose-built concert rooms: the Star Inn in Churchgate and the Millstone Inn in Crown Street.[1]

The Star Concert Room began life in connection with the Millstone Inn, established there by the proprietor, Thomas Sharples, in 1832. It must have been a great success, for in 1840 Sharples transferred the name, along with his own managerial talent, to extensive new premises attached to the Old Cock Inn in Churchgate, which became the Star Inn, but which under its old name had been notorious for holding cockfights. So, what became Bolton's main centre of working-class entertainment for over half a century started life as a direct response to the growth of beerhouses, and perhaps also as an alternative to cockfighting as a way of attracting customers to a pub. The attractions of the Star had much in common with the sideshows at circuses, wakes and fairs, and it became a sort of permanent version of these, making every weekend a mini-holiday for those who could afford it, and fitting old-established styles of entertainment into the pattern of the industrial working week.

The *Bolton Chronicle* described the Star concert room in 1852:

It stood immediately behind the Star [Inn] and was in three general divisions or stories, — the first, on the ground floor, used for the purposes of a brewhouse, stable, yard, paint-shop, workshops, & c.; the second, the concert-room; and the third, the museum. Above the museum was a promenade, forming, in a great measure, the roof of the building; the south end being distinguished by the mast of a large ship, with a quantity of rigging.

The promenade also exhibited a statue of a Red Indian, a ship's figurehead, a garden and an ornamental pond, and afforded panoramic views of the town. Visitors could have their photograph taken up there by a Mr Benfold, who also kept a 'Temple of Magic' on the lower floor, where he sold magic tricks and demonstrated their secrets to the buyers. The museum below housed an incredible variety of exhibits; entry was free, except on Sundays, but catalogues cost 1*d*. There were waxworks and busts of the famous and notorious, paintings and models of famous scenes, and such items as Napoleon, the Royal Family, Tom Thumb, 'Greeks holding a council of war', 'a celebrated card party which some years ago met at the Ship Inn, Bolton', famous murderers and reconstructions of their deeds and subsequent executions, 'a piece of coal, found with a Toad in it', a model of 'an old monkey teaching a young one to play the violin', a weighing machine, specimens of calligraphy, live monkeys and parrots, and various other live animals. The budget did not quite stretch to more exotic creatures, but there was the next best thing: 'A cat, born entirely without forelegs . . . It jumps around on its hind legs in a manner closely resembling that of a kangaroo'. There was a real leopard for a time, but it had to be put down after it killed its keeper. Sharples saw no reason to let such a famous incident go uncommemorated, and he had the animal stuffed and added to the museum.[2]

The concert hall on the first floor was very large. It measured 150 feet by 45 feet, with a bar below the galleries at one end, the stage at the other, and seats and tables in between. It often held over a thousand people, and as many as 1,500 could be crammed in. The only entrance was through the Star Inn, and admission was by 2*d*. token, which could be redeemed at the bar. A high proportion of the audience, perhaps half, were young factory workers, male and female, but there were also married couples, and groups of working people of all ages. Unlike the Old Theatre, the Star opened on Monday afternoon, which was still 'Saint Monday' for many classes of workers outside the factories, particularly colliers, in the days before the modern weekend came into being. Sharples proudly advertised the Star as 'the oldest [such] establishment outside London', and there seems to be no firm reason to doubt his claim.[3]

The surviving playbills, and the 1847–50 account book, give us a lively picture of the way the Star was run during this period.[4] At different times, the concert room played host to clowns, acrobats on horses, an illuminated tableau of the Great Fire of London, 'A grand magnifico diapatrica, or hydrogen gas phantasmagoria and dissolving views', and to 'Ethiopian Entertainments, in which the sports and pastimes of the coloured race are delineated in a masterly and chaste manner, through the medium of Songs, Refrains and Ditties, as sung by the slaves of the South, at their Merry Meetings, Junketings, Gathering in of the Crops of Sugar and Cotton, & c.'. The more spectacular attractions were punctuated by a whole gallery of more or less eccentric operators — 'Thomas Lang, the Celebrated Mountain Stag, who will take his Surprising Leaps from the ground without the aid of a Spring Board', 'Mons. Gouffe, the Man Monkey', 'Booth, the one-legged jumper', 'Wild's Dog Nelson' and 'Perkins' Patent Steam Gun'. An extract from

Sharples' account book in December 1847 gives us an idea of how he handled the day-to-day running of such a place:

> Put notice in green room for music and singing to be ready to commence at 10 o'clock at Newyear's Day and write a programme to the performances dont have firing or anything else to darken the room — We had no man top of the stone steps to keep folks on the right side would have been better with — There were too many singers — We had no bills, posters or advertisements — but just four walking billboards 1/6 & glass of ale each — We gave Music and Singers paper tickets 4 each so they got a glass when they pleased and they all got drunk nearly dont give them anything till night — Old Sutton got drunk not fit to depend on for a busy time — It was a very sloppy day underfoot deal of snow on the ground — Sunday was so wet no one could turn out — Very few shows and never more folks in the town and think more might have been made of it if we had some new novelty.

Sharples was obviously aware of the commercial possibilities of a well-run concert room, and by New Year's Eve he had his novelty to attract the crowds who came to Bolton for the New Year Fair — a simulation of 'The Great Fire of London'. This was a great success, but the middle of January saw terrible weather and the worst week since the Star was built, for it lost £12. Not to be beaten, he ransacked the props for 'The Great Fire of London' and exhibited the equally spectacular 'Storming of Amoy', publicised by 1,000 bills and 50 posters. Takings rose nearly a half on the previous week. Thomas Sharples clearly knew his audience and was always ready to provide them with what they wanted, as another entry a fortnight later shows:

> Herr and Madame Hist & Son poses Plastiques & Gymnasia £7-0-0 Stop'd £3 for three nights had piece called Man Monkey instead it took very well.

The Star was expensive to run. £1 a night was the standard fee for a good act, while even minor turns such as Booth, the one-legged jumper, earned £2 a week, — more than double the average industrial wage. Every week between three and six different artistes had to be paid, together with the regular band at £26–8s.–6d. a week, the staff, and the 'supernumeries' in any tableaux — 5/- a week for an adult, 6d. a night for a child. The basic running expenses came to some £75 a week, but once this was cleared, most of the rest was profit. Expenses rose on major holidays, such as New Year's week 1849 when the need for extra staff and provisions and a well-peopled 'Fairy Palace' pushed the costs up to £135 — and the takings up to £166. The table below shows the seasonal variation in takings in 1848 (a depressed year) and 1849 (a better one). Takings were on the whole highest in the summer months, when the regular theatre was closed, and there was a very pronounced post-New Year slump, after people had blown all their money on seasonal merriment. In holiday weeks the revenue could be enormous, as in Whit Week 1849, when 3,600 bottles of ginger beer were sold in a single day. Nor did the prolonged trade depression of 1848 leave Sharples at a loss; in December, with trade particularly bad, he hired a lecturer on emigration, who was so successful he was kept on for a second week.

## Table 1. STAR MUSIC HALL, BOLTON

*Average monthly takings, 1848–9*

|           | 1848 | 1849 |
|-----------|------|------|
|           | £    | £    |
| January   | 77*  | 92*  |
| February  | 110  | 100  |
| March     | 102  | 100  |
| April     | NS   | 106* |
| May       | 87   | 109* |
| June      | 119* | 124  |
| July      | 119  | 125  |
| August    | (136)| 122  |
| September | 139  | 121  |
| October   | 103  | 129  |
| November  | 95   | 124  |
| December  | 86*  | NS   |

*The inflated receipts in holiday weeks have been removed from the figures of months marked with an asterisk because they distort the general trend. Each figure is based on at least two weeks' takings and usually four, except for August 1848, when only one week was available.

| *Takings in public holiday weeks*           | £   |
|---------------------------------------------|-----|
| New Year week 27.12 – 2.1 1847/8            | 165 |
| Following week 3.1 – 9.1.1848               | 164 |
| Whit week 12 June–18 June 1848              | 226 |
| Christmas week 1848, 25 Dec–30 Dec          | 105 |
| New Year week 1849, 1–7 January             | 261 |
| Easter Week 1849, 9–15 April                | 166 |
| Whit Week 1849, 28 May–3 June               | 246 |

The Star's success rankled with many rival publicans, and it was they, rather than reformers, who mounted the first campaign against the Star. In August 1842, a number of them formed an 'anti-singing saloon association', which chose the alleged 'demoralising effect' of 'that overgrown institution' as its point of attack. A member of the association wrote to the *Bolton Chronicle* complaining about monkeys being exhibited there on Sundays, and claiming that when the Star was full, the crowds in the street outside had sometimes to be held back by a man with a whip. The publicans gained the support of the vicar of Bolton, Canon Slade, whose long-standing links with old-fashioned Toryism in Bolton had no doubt made him a friend of the drink interest. In 1843 he led a successful campaign to get the Star's application for a licence to perform stage plays under the new Theatres'

Act turned down. The following year, Thomas Sharples and Finley Frazer (proprietor of a similar but smaller establishment) found their drink licences temporarily suspended because they opened their museums and allowed music in their houses on Sundays. Sharples closed the menagerie part of his museum on the next Sunday as a gesture of good faith, and the licences were returned; in future, however, the museum remained shut on Sundays.[5]

Thomas Sharples, in fact, knew he had to cultivate the magistrates, some of whom owned rival pubs, especially when the influential vicar sided with the drink interest. Privately, Sharples probably did this using his Freemason connections. His son William, who took over from him in 1850, immediately advertised the good character of the Star:

### THE CONCERT ROOM

Is a resort principally for the working-classes who, after their daily labour, can here enjoy a couple of hours in a manner suited exactly to their taste. Here a thousand of hardworking and industrious persons may be seen together, listening attentively and appreciating Music, Singing and other novelties; where immorality is studiously avoided. Youths are strictly refused admittance to the concert room, whether attended by their parents or not.

The Star was, he proudly proclaimed, 'under the patronage of the working classes' — a dig at the Old Theatre, which sometimes advertise its performances as 'under the patronage of' local dignitaries, but whose poor quality presentations were notorious. (Nevertheless, Sharples was happy enough to announce Joseph Crook, the local Tory MP, as patron in 1852.) Finley Frazer, answering criticism in the press, went even further in his claims for the virtues of concert rooms:

It has often been my lot to witness persons, certainly not of the richest cultivation of mind, drawn from the use of low and vulgar language, and, indeed riotous conduct, into some submission after hearing a good sentimental song. The heart, as it were by magic spell, becomes subdued, and the baser feelings and passions give way to more sublime thoughts and actions.

The softly-softly approach (though perhaps not Frazer's rather heavy-footed version of it) seems to have had some success. Religious Dissenters, who led the movement for moral improvement which later proved to be the Star's greatest threat, were doubtless wary of siding with the reactionary Canon Slade and the drink interest. Sharples and Frazer were actually defended for their licences in 1844 by John Taylor, the lawyer and amateur actor, who in later years made a point of turning up at every annual licensing sessions to oppose the granting of any new drink licences at all. He claimed then on Sharples's behalf that many sober and well-dressed citizens who had come a long way to see the menagerie were disappointed to find it shut, and argued further that 'the sole purpose of Mr Sharples's demanding a penny for admission [on Sundays] was to maintain the respectability of his company'. Despite being something of a circus attraction, the Star museum did have its more 'rational' element, which was much more evident in Finley Frazer's collection of butterflies and insects.[6] Enthusiastic working-class hobbyists were probably not too fussy about the 'tone' of such places. Perhaps Taylor, whose amateur acting gave him a broader outlook on life than many of his fellow-reformers, saw in the early museums the germ of something better emerging, in that 'age of improvement', from the world of the pub.

In July 1852 the whole Star complex was burnt down, causing between six and seven thousand pounds' worth of damage and throwing some fifty people out of work. With the annual brewster sessions hardly a month away, the critics pounced and there was a furious battle over whether the Star's licence should be renewed.[7] This time, though, the battle lines were differently drawn. Over the previous few years, vigorous teetotal campaigning directed towards the ultimate end of getting all Bolton's pubs closed down had clearly frightened off the drink interest from joining this new campaign, which was directed against all pub singing saloons and not just against the Star. Canon Slade was also conspicuously absent from the ranks of the critics, which were dominated by Nonconformists and Sunday school teachers. They saw the Star as the worst amongst a number of bogeys designed as 'pernicious traps' to seduce Sunday scholars into a life of waste and debauchery. A crowded public meeting heard a description of the place by a Baptist minister who had visited it 'on an ordinary occasion':

> There were at least a thousand persons present, most of them were from twelve to twenty-five years of age. The place was so crowded that the waiters were unable to walk upon the floor, and were therefore hopping about among the heads of the people on the backs of the seats, handing to them pipes of tobacco, and various kinds of drink and spiritous liquors. Young people of both sexes were huddled together in the closest contact, and most of them appeared to be freely using the spiritous provisions of the bar. While looking on, a slight skirmish took place between two persons in the middle of the room, which caused great excitement and cries of 'turn him out', &c. &c. In the middle of this uproar, a tall well-dressed female came onto the platform, and attracted their attention by a song. I do not say that the song was immoral, but I do affirm that the gestures of the lady who sang it, together with the stimulating influence of the drink and the whole scene, were calculated to excite the basest passions of the human mind . . . My heart sickened at what I heard . . . I felt that I was in the very suburbs of hell.

*facing page*

Fig. 11   By 1843, the Bolton Theatre was trying to attract the popular audience from the music halls by using melodramas. At the same time, it was trying to win back the lucrative middle-class audience, which had largely turned from the theatre to more respectable entertainments, by trumpeting the moral lessons to be drawn from the plays.

Fig. 12   The Star Inn Concert Room seems to have been renamed the Royal Arena for this presentation in aid of the Bolton dispensary. The Star was clearly trying to curry favour with influential people here, partly because of a forthcoming application for a licence to perform stage plays under the new Theatres Act (which was turned down) and partly as a defence against an 'anti-singing saloon association', formed by rival publicans the previous year. The circus was still respectable, and items such as the 'Roman Wrestlers' and 'Sports of Bye Gone Days' were calculated to appeal to different middle-class tastes. The bill, although not typical of the Star, none the less gives some idea of the range of popular entertainment offered there in this period.

56

11

# THEATRE, BOLTON.

### Licensed by the Court of Quarter Sessions.

## Shrove Tuesday !

### A HOLIDAY TREAT.

#### TWO TRAGEDIES IN ONE EVENING !!!

## THIS PRESENT TUESDAY,

**FEBRUARY THE 28th, 1843,**

The Performances will commence with LILLO'S celebrated domestic Tragedy of

# GEORGE BARNWELL;

### OR

## The London Merchant.

*The moral tragedy of this play cannot be better exemplified than by the following Extract from the Journal of Mr. Ross, the actor, to a Friend.*

In the year 1752, during the Christmas holidays, I played **George Barnwell**, and the late Mrs. Pritchard, **Millwood**; Dr. Barrowby, Physician in St. Bartholomew's Hospital, was sent for by a young gentleman in Gt. St. Helen's, apprentice to an eminent merchant. He found him so very ill that no medicine could touch. The doctor told his patient he was certain there was something oppressed him, and that it would be in vain to render him medicine unless he would open his mind freely : the youth, at last, confessed he had been entrusted with cash, which he had made free with, to the amount of £200. That going two or three nights before to Drury Lane, to see **GEORGE BARNWELL**, he was so forcibly struck, that he had not enjoyed a moment's peace since, and that he resolved, it it would please providence to raise a friend to extricate him out of that distress, to dedicate the rest of his life to religion and virtue. The doctor undertook to reconcile him to his father and friends, and to replace the sum embezzled. The young man's peace of mind became reinstated, and he lived to be a very considerable merchant. Though I never knew the young man's name, nor saw him, I received, for many year's, at my benefit, a note sealed up, with ten guineas, & these words, "**A tribute of gratitude from one who was so highly obliged, and saved from ruin, by seeing Mr. Ross's performance of GEORGE BARNWELL.**"

**POPE** was amongst the distinguished characters who had the curiosity to be present at the first performance of **George Barnwell**, and he commended it much. He observed that the fable was well conducted, the diction natural, or it at times it was elevated something above the simplicity of the characters, it never deceded to meanness, or departed from the truth of style calculated to reach the heart.

| | | | |
|---|---|---|---|
| Thorogood | Mr. FISHER | Constable | Mr. MARTIN |
| George Barnwell | Mr. CHAMBERLAIN | Footman | Mr. WILLIAMS |
| Freeman | Mr. MONTAGUE | | |
| Uncle to Barnwell | Mr. SIMEON | Millwood | Mrs. FISHER |
| Blunt | Mr. HAYES | Maria | Mrs. SIMEON |
| Jailor | Mr. WATSON | Lucy | Mrs. MONTAGUE |

## COMIC SONG, BY MR. HAYES.

### OVERTURE BY THE BAND, CONDUCTED BY MR. RIBBON.

## COMIC SONG, BY MR. FISHER.

To conclude with ROWES celebrated Pathetic and beautifully poetic Tragedy of

# JANE SHORE;

## THE UNHAPPY FAVOURITE.

| | | | |
|---|---|---|---|
| Duke of Gloster | Mr. BATTIE | Belmour | Mr. MARTIN |
| Lord Hastings | Mr. BEAUCHAMP | Derby | Mr. WATSON |
| Dumont | Mr. CHAMBERLAIN | Porter | Mr. JONES |
| Rateliff | Mr. SIMEON | Jane Shore | Mrs. WATSON |
| Catesby | Mr. MONTAGUE | Alicia | Mrs. FISHER |

## Boxes, 2s.; Pit, 1s.; Gallery, 6d.

☞ Doors to be open at Half-past six and the Performances to commence at seven precisely:

HALF-PRICE WILL BE TAKEN TO THE BOXES AT NINE O'CLOCK.

*On Wednesday Evening, the Tragedy of Brutus, and other Entertainments, being for the BENEFIT OF MR. PRESTON, and the Last Night of his Engagement.*

The Manager is happy to announce, he has formed an arrangement with that celebrated Performer,

## Mr. BUTLER,

Of the Theatres Royal, Drury Lane and Covent Garden ; and principal Tragedian of the Theatre Royal, Manchester :—

### FOR ONE NIGHT ONLY.

#### ON THURSDAY, Sheridan Knowles',

## TRAGEDY OF "VIRGINIUS,"

The part of Virginius, by Mr. BUTLER. (His first appearance in Bolton.)

☞ Caution—Persons are cautioned against Purchasing or Receiving Checks at the Doors, as none but the original possessor will be re-admitted.

The Scenic Department under the Direction of MR BATTIE—Machinist.......... MR W THOMAS

**Stage Manager** .......... MR T. TAYLOR.

HARGREAVES PRINTER, FOLDS-STREET, BOLTON.

Fig. 12

FOR THE BENEFIT OF THE BOLTON DISPENSARY.

Grand Morning Performance, on Friday, March 31st commencing at 2 o'clock

# ROYAL ARENA

### STAR INN, BOLTON.

## GRAND DAY PERFORMANCE,

### AND

### Juvenile Entertainments.

#### ON FRIDAY NEXT, MARCH 31st, 1843,

Commencing at 2 o'clock

## FOR THE BENEFIT OF THE BOLTON Dispensary.

The public of Bolton are respectfully informed, that Mr. SHARPLES, at a great expense has secured the services of the following Artists. In order to make the entertainments as attractive as possible

## LE PETITE DUCROW,

The wonder of the world

## Mr. T. MOSELEY,

### AND

## SIGNOR BOTTARI,

The first horsemen of the present day, from DUCROW'S NATIONAL ESTABLISHMENT !!!

The Gates of the Arena will be thrown open precisely at 2 o'clock when the

## PET PONY, MATCHLESS,

Will be put through his various performances, as trained by Mr. T. JONES.

To be followed by a principal act of Horsemanship by

## SIGNOR BOTTARI,

### On a Bareback'd Steed.

After which a new piece, introducing the Juvenile branches of the Establishment entitled the

## MORNING STAR,

Sprite, Gaily mounted on his flying Courser.......... Mr. E. HEMMING

Mischievous Nymphs.......... Masters HEMMING, PARKE, and Miss WOODWARD

To be continued by

## Mr. T. MOSELEY'S

UNRIVALLED ACT OF HORSEMANSHIP,

Representing characters of England, Ireland, and Scotland.

## THE 3 SWISS BROTHERS

Will appear and go through their unrivalled performances, forming pictures of the ANCIENT & GRAND CLASSICAL GROUPINGS.

## LE PETITE DUCROW,

### THE WONDER OF THE AGE,

Will appear on his Rapid Steed, as the

## IRISH BOY,

Rival Clowns.......... Messrs. SWANN & JONES

The whole to conclude with a new piece, with new Dresses, entitled the

## Days of Queen Elizabeth ;

### OR, SPORTS OF BYE GONE DAYS.

Introducing the whole of the company, Male and Female.

King...Mr. Cullen  Queen...Mrs. W. Hemming  Knight of the Lion ...Mr. R. Hemming  Knight of the Crest...Mr. E. Hemming  Knight of the Sun ... Mr. Clarke  Knight of the Black Plume.......... Mr. T. Jones

Ladies of the Court.......... Mrs. R. Hemming and  Mrs. Jones

Royal Pages...Masters Hemming & Parke,  Miss Woodward,  & the Infant Prince C. & B. Russell  Court Jester ...Mr. Swann  Royal Herald .......... Mr. W. HEMMING

Roman Gladiators.......... Messrs. Russell, Dipple, and Russell

Hodge, a valiant Miller ...Mr D. Jones  Lapstone, a courageous Shoemaker.......... Mr. Lee  Birk, a gay young Country Lad........Mr. Richards  Blackhead.......... Mr. Parish

Madge, wife to Lapstone...Mrs. Chapman  Margery, the Miller's wife... Mrs. R. Hemming

INCIDENTAL TO THE PIECE,

## FEATS BY THE ROMAN WRESTLERS,

Four seasons of the year, Spring, Summer, Autumn, and Winter, Emblematic signs of England, Ireland and Scotland, with characteristic Dances. Introduction of the Mountain Shepherd. The Old English MORRIS DANCERS.—Sports in the Sun—Hurling the Dart—Tilting—Wrestling—Quarter Laff Fighting, etc. (HARGREAVES, PRINTER.)

Price of Admission to the Galleries, 1s. To the Body of the Boxes, 6d.—Children half-price.

The rapid quelling of the fight by popular pressure and swift stage management, and the fact that many of the youngsters would have been drinking minerals, suggests a hectic but well-ordered evening, but the reformers objected on principle to 'sensual gratification' and the stirring of 'base passions.' In addition, a lot of evidence was adduced from local youngsters imprisoned in Manchester and Liverpool. These reports as quoted at the meeting painted a black picture of the Star as the centre of a juvenile crime ring, with children resorting to theft to get money for admission, selling their goods to a network of local receivers. Unfortunately, none of these testimonies survive in full, but we do have some similar confessions taken from Bolton youths in Salford House of Correction in 1859–60 which are clearly similar.[8] These are often stilted and lurid — 'The Star Inn is the greatest evil in Bolton, and that I knew anywhere'; 'I should never have been here were it not for the Star Inn' — but the picture they give of juvenile life rings true. One seventeen-year-old Bolton boy, assistant to a bolt-maker, told his interviewer how his mother had died when he was nine, and how when he was 14 he and his elder sister had left their drunken, violent father:

> I got into bad company before I left my father — 4 months — one Richard Bolton, 17, John Glone, 15, Henry Bolton, 12, older than me, took me to spend my School wage, they were Carters for their father and took me in their Cart. They took me to the Star Inn, and to the Mill Stone, the latter now made in a Concert Room and Dancing Room. The Craven Heifer, Benjamin Laws on Bolton Moor is another Dancing place. I used to go errands to my Uncle to buy leather, and I got the money. Richard Bolton and his brother used to persuade me to go to the Star with them and spend 5/– and 6/– many a time with them at the Star out of Uncle's money. Used to get Pies, Tarts, Fruit, Pop — if you get Ale when the Act is over, you go down, and get half a gallon or gallon [sic], and pay so much on the bottle, if a quart bottle 4d for it, 4d for the ale. I was then about 13, going to Can Row School . . . Sister told me many a time not to go — she has taken my money out of my pocket on my going to bed to prevent me going. She now works at Crooks. I went every night of the week, but chiefly Friday and Saturday. Left my work 5 and 6 days together to go to the Star and Circuses with the Boltons, and they have left their Carts, putting up their horses, when their Father did not know but they were carting Flags for the town . . . This Star Inn has been both their ruin and mine.

The story smacks more of the evils of neglecting and exploiting children than of the evils of music and alcohol, but the reformers had the Star firmly in their sights as the open plughole of Bolton's sink of iniquity, creating currents that drew in the human flotsam and jetsam of the town. One Dissenting minister saw in the temptations of youth by the singing saloons a metaphor for the original Fall of Man, while another linked Britain's industrial progress with her moral progress and saw singing saloons as a threat to both:

> We prided ourselves, as a nation, in our greatness. But what was it that had helped to place Great Britain on the proud pre-eminence she occupied amongst the nations of the world? He ventured to say that one great means that he contributed to Britain's moral pre-eminence was the influence of the Sunday schools in the land (applause). But here was a power now in operation among the people, which (and he hoped he would not be

58

charged with a hasty or strong impression) he believed had its origins from hell (hear, hear), among the agents of darkness, which was one great means of contributing to the demoralising and blighting influences exerted upon the public around us.

The teachers of St George's Sunday school went so far as to cast themselves in the role of their patron saint, slaying the dragon of iniquity. An almost millenarian temper ran through the meeting, as if those present felt they were averting some sort of social apocalypse. Pubs, it was argued, had once been useful resorts of weary travellers, but, thanks to the new roads and railways, they had outlived their useful life; they were now becoming 'hotbeds of evil' which had no place in a civilised society. The actual resolution passed, though, was aimed more at the magistrates than at posterity; it called for 'a more stringent application of the law' relating to places of entertainment.

The magistrates reacted to this campaign by suspending the licences only of the Star and the Millstone. It was immediately alleged that at least one of them owned a rival pub whose tenant had been complaining of the competition, and that the magistrates concerned, as Liberals, had shown partiality by failing to suspend the licence of the Liberal owner of another large concert room. William Sharples (who had now taken over from his father) stayed in the background during the ensuing controversy, stoically playing the part of one wronged, and left the mud-slinging to his acting manager at the Star, George Gray, a self-styled 'historical lecturer and dramatic author'. Writing to the *Bolton Chronicle*, Gray attacked 'those ignorant self-glorifiers who see nothing in the public house but drunkenness and obscenity':

> I wish to know if any one will object to a poor man having a glass of ale and having his song? I believe not. The wiser plan will be to take care that he is cheated in neither his ale or his song . . . It is impossible to 'pooh, pooh' down these multitudes or drive them away by a policeman.

He had no truck with artificial 'rational' recreations, and denounced free parks and libraries as 'mischievous absurdities', seeing commercial entertainments such as concert rooms and stage plays as 'the only means of conveying instruction on a large scale'. Yet what was happening? The established theatre had forfeited its popularity with the new mass audience because its operators, 'clinging to old habits and prejudices' about the need for high-class audiences, ended up only being able to afford to put on trash most of the time. The concert rooms were unable to step in and restore standards because they were refused theatrical licences by prejudiced authorities:

> The obvious result is that the proprietors are forced upon minor performances of songs, tumblings, & c., which, though in themselves harmless enough, are not calculated for the purposes of intellectual elevation.

Gray admitted that some youngsters did get into the Star, but (in his evidence to the Select Committee on Public Houses the following year) he had an answer for those critics of this who also harped on about the virtues of industry:

If the boys are able to go into the mills and factories to earn their living, and are made premature men of in that way, I submit to this Committee the gross injustice of excluding them from their amusements in the evenings.[9]

He also adopted the rhetoric of 'rational recreation' in defending the role of these amusements in an industrial town, writing of 'the hardworking mechanic in the saloon made cheerful after his day of labour, and sent with renewed spirit to his morning toil'. Other writers to the *Bolton Chronicle* supported the view that the singing saloon was on the whole more orderly and better-run than the pub:

In Singing Saloons I find the working man spending his evening for a trifle, and not unfrequently with the partner of his life watching over him, and preventing, by her presence, his indulging in excess, were he so inclined, at the same time enjoying the same pleasure as himself . . . In the Singing Saloon the poor man may have his ginger beer without being served with reluctance and being pointed at as an oddity . . . there is no card, dominoes, draughts, bagatelle, & c., playing, causing drink to be won and lost, and afterwards 'to be drunk on the premises' . . . Better hours are kept at Singing Saloons than is the case in a general way at other places . . .

The *Bowtun Loominary* put the case in its own inimitable way:

Aw know one thing, wurchin foak will ha their amusements; they wur made to laf as weel as cry; un it doesn't need a philosopher to tell us which does um th'moast good. Aw know there is a set of foak as wonders why they should be so fond o lowfin . . . But, thank God we're not aw cast in the same square shaped mould.

The magistrates met a month later to reconsider their decision to suspend the licences of the Star and Millstone. The Superintendent of Police appeared as a character reference for William Sharples, and it emerged that no formal complaint had been laid against either institution (not surprising, since off-duty police were among the regular customers). The magistrates, perhaps embarrassed by the allegations of partiality and by the obvious feeling in favour of the two proprietors who had been deprived of their livelihoods, restored the licences. In the end, popular demand found the support to make itself felt. Bolton's frustrated Sunday school teachers and reformers turned their hand to other things. The next year's unsuccessful campaign was to force the Sunday closing of pubs, and it revealed not so much a well of agonised concern over the moral fate of Bolton's innocent youth as a deep vein of hostility to all unregenerate forms of working-class amusement. There were near-riots over their proposals, but the temperance campaigners proved to be slow learners, and twenty years later their speakers were still provoking violent hostility in Bolton by insulting the intelligence and tastes of their working-class audiences.[10] The 1852 controversy, though, brought demands for positive alternative entertainments rather than mere repressiveness, helping the growth of the movement for 'rational recreation' which we have already observed. Meanwhile, however, the Star was being rebuilt, and it soon found again a regular place in working-class life far stronger than that of any of the 'improving' pastimes promoted by the middle class.

*Notes*
1.  See above, Chapter 4, 'Drink and Society', and the evidence of George Wolstenholme and George Gray, SC on Public Houses 1852–3, pp. 247–59 and 443–56.
2.  *BC* 17.7.1852, 24.7.1852; *Bolton Almanac* 1852, p. xv; Star Inn Museum Catalogues, 1845 and (?) 1859/61, *BRL* B506 (what appears to be an accompanying leaf to the latter is filed under B 792); Taylor, *Autobiography*, p. 120; Greenhalgh MSS; *BC* 17.10.1844.
3.  The question is really one of definitions. Nothing is known of what the original Star concert room attached to the Millstone Inn was like, but its 1832 founding date places it ahead of the several working-class pub concert rooms established in London in the 1830s. These resembled the Star as it was between 1840 and 1852, when it had a raised gallery around three sides, but ordinary chairs and tables on the floor, and a stage. For Harold Scott (*The Early Doors* (London, 1946), Chapter 2, esp. pp. 52–3) the addition of the gallery at the back signals the advent of 'music hall', although as he describes it, the gallery originally existed to provide a separate 'saloon bar' for wealthier patrons and only later became a working-class presence. The Star was always working-class throughout, and until 1852 had a single bar below the rear gallery. From at least the late 1840s the gallery was more expensive than the floor, and by 1859 it had its own bar. Here, however, we are on uncertain ground, for the Star had more than one hall at this time — see appendix. For Bailey (*op. cit.*, Chapter 7), charging admission, rather than simply a 'refreshment check' or 'wet money' (redeemable for drink) seems to be the criterion for music hall, as opposed to pub, entertainment. Following C. D. Stuart and A. J. Park ('The Variety Stage' (London, 1895)) he identifies the Oxford, in London's Oxford Street, as 'the first true music hall', in 1861. Again, uncertainty appears, but the Star seems to have operated on the 'refreshment check' system until 1852, and on a mixture of 'wet money' and (at least for the 6d. seats) straight admission money from 1855. But whatever the details, the Star had every appearance of being a successful working-class music hall in the 1850s, if not before; on Easter Monday 1849, nearly half the takings seem to have come from entrance money ('settle') and the gallery supplement.
4.  *BRL* ZZ/82 1843/9, 1843/22; adverts in *BC*, e.g. 26.9.1846, 20.4.1844, 28.9.1844; Star Inn Account Book 1847–50, *BRL*. Unfortunately, Sharples did not keep up the detail of this first entry. He had headed the book 'Day Book' and seems to have intended it originally as a series of business memos to himself as well as just an account book — a sign of careful management.
5.  *BC* 22.10.1842, 10.12.–24.12.1842, 28.9.1844; Bailey, *op. cit.*, p. 19. Sunday music at the Star was not banned in 1843, as Bailey states; it was continued until 1873, when pressure from the magistrates forced the manager to end the practice.
6.  *Bolton Almanac* 1850, p. xv; *BC* 22.10.1842, 28.9.1844, 10.7.1852. Frazer's collection of insects was sold in 1870 (*BC* 3.9.70).
7.  *BC* 14.8.–9.10.1852; *Era* 29.8–9.10.1852; all cited by Bailey, *op. cit.*, pp. 19–20 and 31–2. Copies of the newspaper material are lodged in *BRL*, along with other material relating to the Star.
8.  'Depositions relating to the Star Inn . . . Bolton' (*BRL*).
9.  Select Committee on Public Houses, *PP* 1852–3 xxxvii, pp. 443–56, e.g. Q7799.
10. See the long version of this study in *BRL*, 'Drink and Society' section.

# 7
# The Growth of Music Hall in Bolton, 1855–1900

The 1850s saw a take-off in the growth of music hall in England, and Bolton was well in the forefront of this. In the autumn of 1854 a revamped and enlarged Millstone concert room was opened, anticipating by a few months the re-opening of the Star on New Year's Day 1855. By 1857 the Star Concert Hall had become the Theatre Royal, while a fresh concert room had been added which was soon renamed the Museum Music Hall when Sharples opened another museum on the site. The occasion, at Christmas 1858, was marked by a free dinner for 200 old ladies from the area, including one woman of 103 — a custom continued for several years after. The exhibits in the new museum were very similar to those in the old one, with portrayals of famous murderers and their notorious deeds very much in evidence. A new bagatelle room adjoined the museum, and the Star also offered hearty meals every lunchtime for 1/– and rooms for the night, which no doubt served many of the visitors to the various amusements, who sometimes came considerable distances. The Angel Inn next door, renamed the Museum Vaults, was added to the property in 1862 to complete a huge entertainment complex consisting of two pubs, a theatre, a music hall, a museum, a games' room and a brewery. J. P. Weston took over the management of the site in 1860–3. He was already well-known locally as an actor, and his wife and daughter as actresses, so the important asset (lacked by the Old Theatre) of a stable and continuous management, closely in touch with local conditions, was preserved. When he sold the place in 1877, the Theatre Royal after successive renovations held 2,500 people and the Museum Music Hall another 1,200. The annual rental value of the site was claimed to be £1,400; £300 for the brewery, £500 for the museum and music hall, and £600 for the Theatre, which could be let for between £12 a week (in summer) and £20 a week (in winter).[1]

The Theatre Royal and the Museum Music Hall were run in different ways. The Theatre ran in seasons, hosting a mixture of visiting companies and home-grown productions, pantomimes and musical comedies. These, however, often acted as vehicles for all sorts of popular sketches and attractions. In 1859, for example, the management contrived to work into a production of 'Babes in the Wood', 'A New Scene, representing the DECK OF A MAN OF WAR, manned by sixty children' (cheaper than using adults), as well as a guest appearance by the ever-popular 'original MAN MONKEY'. In 1857 the theatre offered 'The interesting and exciting drama of the Sea of Ice, with all its novel scenic and mechanical effects'. Some productions espoused a popular political conservatism, such as the 1872 pantomime, 'Jack the Giant Killer', which found time to praise some of the local gentry (including the Tory MP Stephen Blair, a supporter of the Star and one-time leading director in the Bolton Concert Hall Company), and to attack militant coalminers. But a character called Podge, in a scene in an inn, also railed against inequality, at least so far as it entered the new Public House Act:

This closing act was never meant, I'm sure,
To serve the rich man, and turn out the poor . . .
We must obey the laws, both poor and rich,
And laws should make no difference, which or which,
At ten the Parliament has closed our pubs;
At ten the Parliament should close your clubs.

Fairly high prices were charged in the Theatre Royal, even in the slack summer season, as J. P. Weston explained to critics:

Five out of every six companies which usually travel during the summer season will not appear at any theatre where other than what is technically termed 'legitimate' prices obtain, namely — a sixpenny gallery, and a shilling, or ninepenny, pit.

These higher prices doubtless helped the Theatre to keep up with the fashion for increasingly spectacular staging and effects.[2]

The Museum Music Hall retained its 2$d$. entrance fee and may even have moved down-market over the years to complement the more extravagant Theatre Royal next door. The *Bowtun Loominary* applauded the re-opening of the Star Concert Room (as it then still was) on New Year's Day 1855, with a bill of:

Bravura and Ballad-Singing; Gymnastic and Calisthenic Feats; Tight-Rope Dancing; Instrumental Music, with sol performances; Comic Duets and Songs; Hornpipe, etc.; Dancing; Splendid Scenery, Properties and Appointments; A numerous and efficient band.

The magazine described a visit to this opening night by 'Titus Baw' who followed an excited crowd into the sixpenny seats. Looking below, he sees 'Ailse-o-Betty's, a bot of a love o mine' in the cheaper seats; he calls her up, pays the difference for her, and they sit and watch the performance:

. . .Th' next performer wur a yung [sic] lady dancin' on th'tight rope. Hoo beawnced abeawt like a bottle cork, un did aw sorts o balancin' feats, mitch to my astonishment; un Ailse wur so amazed that huw geet hur meawth oppen un couldn't shut it ogen, till th'lady browth hur capers to an end . . . While th'yung lady wur recoverin hur woint, an *owd* foo cawd *Yung*, coom forrud, un begun o tawkin to a chap wi a whip, un he crackt aw sorts o jokes. He axt if this mon wi a whip could tehh him wot two beins thoose wur ut wouldn't work? Says he, the two beins ut winnot work, are a *pig* and a *policeman*. There happent to be a peeler or two in at th'time, un that mended th'joke. Aw lowft awm shure, till they might ha yerd me i'Deighnsgate, un Ailse roared till hoo'd sitch a stitch in hur side, that hoo wur forced to get a sharp glass o gin to rip it eawt . . . By this time th'place wur gettin pratty full, un nearly every chops had a grin on it.

This sympathetic sketch of the Star (clearly intended to be read by some of its audience) included a brief defence of the morals of the place, and characteristically, Staton let his characters speak for themselves:

Aw says to one youth . . . Wot's aw this hurreawin' for?

Waw, he says, we're so fain to see th'Star oppen ogen, that we're just getting shut of a bit of eawr surplus emoshun.

Oh, aw says, aw see, yoar oppenin yoar safety valves, just to prevent yoa fro bastin.

Aye, that's it, he says . . .[3]

Five years later, a thirteen-year-old Irish boy from Bolton described the music hall to the Chaplain of Salford prison:

They act plays — Othello etc., then some singing, then Jack Shepperd, performed sometimes by a man, sometimes by a woman. A lot of lads will bring large Bottles of ale, stone bottles, which will last all night, from half past 6 to 1 o'clock, and will drink, parties of 10 or 20, and curse and swear, some drunk, and others not, who yet will drink as much as those who are drunk. Seen many a score women in the side boxes drunk. I have gone out before the first piece is over, when they have begun to be sick. There's many a score Colliers there now while we are talking about it, Monday 1 o'clock. Fighting in the Gallery and Boxes and Pit — shouting and leaping over the Benches. Very indecent talk — many a thing I would not like to hear again — they fight all roads — sometimes there will be a Policeman or two — but they won't come there on duty, they would not take a man up who was seen picking pockets . . . There are always as many as 100 little boys waiting outside, waiting for persons going out, who will say, give me your ticket and I'll give you a penny for it — they will go in with it and say they have been up afore . . . They think nothing of lying, and the check taker will ask them what was performing, the boys get their answer ready from those who have come out. Very many of the little boys get liquor. They won't let very little boys go into the Museum.

The boys would then cram into the already crowded gallery. The constant crush of youngsters wanting to get in seems to have made the management more willing to admit them over the years, as a 45-year-old man in the same prison noted. He also decribed how the nature of the performance affected the licensing arrangements in the Star:

The mode of getting liquor is from below [i.e. the pub]. When it is a singing room, it is then brought up to you. When it is used as a Theatre [in the legal sense] you must fetch it yourself . . . You can get liquor on the same landing as the Pits, upstairs, about 30 yards off, and also below. It is higher than the Chapel gallery of this prison. I have seen scores of times, more boys than any other class, climbing up and down from one part to another, quite little children. At one time, years ago, this was not allowed, but now Sharples takes money from any age.[4]

J. P. Weston, who became manager of the music hall about three years later, tightened up on this, although he still freely admitted to the magistrates when applying for a licence for it in 1873 that boys of 14 were allowed in. However, he also adduced several policemen, including the Chief Constable of Bolton, to testify to the good order of the Museum Music Hall. One Sergeant described how:

He had been there a full hundred times, and he had never seen anything immoral or indecent, or calculated to offend, from any of the performers or singers . . . If there was any disturbance, it was soon quieted. The hall was frequented by decent people . . .[5]

64

During the 1860s and 1870s, the chairman at the Museum was J. B. Geoghegan, who also wrote comic songs, and was later manager himself. He lived in the Angel Inn with a large family, and many years later, a nephew and one of his daughters remembered how the old Museum was. The cheaper rows of seats had ledges on the back to rest beer mugs on, while the boxes were equipped with simple cane seats with anti-macasser backs. There were two bars, one for the 2*d*. and 4*d*. seats, and one for the 6*d*. seats. Geoghegan's style as chairman was vigorous. From his box at the side of the stage he would take the part of the audience against a bad performer, shouting, 'you're no good! You'll be paid up tonight!'. However, he discouraged bad language, and if a fight started he would wade in and eject the troublemakers. The stage itself was of the proscenium type, dimly lit by gas, and with only a few props. The orchestra was a good deal smaller than that at the old Star in the 1840s — just a piano, a cornet and a violin. Performances lasted from 7.30 until 10 p.m., which left an hour before time for singing round the piano at the back of the hall, giving this extensive place all the conviviality of a simple pub.[6]

## Threats and Competition

The Museum Music Hall and the Theatre Royal had to face a number of challenges between the 1850s and the 1880s: attacks from reformers and magistrates; attempts by temperance reformers to stage cheap, wholesome and non-alcoholic alternatives; and competition from other commercial institutions. It survived them all.

The temperance movement still saw the re-opened Star as 'the means of sending more souls to hell than the Sunday schools of Bolton are the means of preventing from going thither', but in general a more constructive spirit than earlier seems to have prevailed. The re-opening was accompanied by a series of 'Concerts for the People', organised in connection with the Mechanics' Institute at the Temperance Hall. Tickets sold for as little as 3*d*. and were available from many of the same bookshops and other outlets which sold tickets for theatrical performances in the town. The first of this series of 'cheap and popular entertainments to while away the long winter evenings' was a 'vocal and pictorial' story entitled: 'The Far West, or the Emigrant's Progress from the Old World to the New; and Negro Life in Freedom and Slavery'. It had a moral, but it was not very different from the offerings of the commercial theatre; even the more sedate songs and recitals at these concerts partook of the fashion for popular variety, and 1*d*. songsheets were issued at ticket outlets, although they also stemmed from the widespread prejudice against drama. This prejudice could be taken to absurd lengths; three years later the Temperance Hall offered the whole of 'Macbeth' staged as a recital with piano accompaniment — hardly likely to appeal to Bolton's 'gallery gods'.[7] Numerous organisations, including 'improving' institutions and the temperance lobby, joined in the fashion for 'Penny Readings' in the late 1850s and early 1860s; these seem to have been designed to raise money as much as to attract people to the road of self-improvement. They were very popular for a time, although the audience would often rush out to the nearest pubs during the interval.[8] The

65

Temperance Hall kept up its entertainments long after penny readings had become rather a stale joke, gaining a music licence in 1873 (along with the Co-Operative Hall and, in 1876, the Good Templars' Hall), and was even licensed as a music hall for a time around 1895. Still later, in 1900, the Methodists opened their Victoria Hall in Knowsley Street — still a concert venue today — with a 'popular concert', and optimistically followed it up with a lecture on the life of the seventeenth-century 'Pilgrim', John Bunyan. The Temperance Hall never opened, like the Museum, on 'Saint Monday' afternoon, but it did begin opening on the official half-holidays on Wednesday and Saturday.[9]

William Sharples and his successor, J. P. Weston, were always careful to keep on the right side of the authorities, exactly as far as was necessary. Cheap seats were offered to school parties for some of the more 'educational' offerings, such as 'Henry Smith's Voyage and Wanderings in America'. In 1859 the Theatre Royal gave a benefit for the newly-formed Ragged School, of which both Sharples and J. T. Staton, 'edditur' of the *Bowtun Loominary*, were patrons. Quite an array of local councillors attended, including the respected Liberal Robert Heywood, but another Liberal, the cotton spinner James Barlow, led a predictable moralistic outcry against such an 'inappropriate' method of fund-raising. The *Loominary* leapt to the defence:

> It's awlus gloomy weather wi sitch men as Mestur Berlow. He has no faith ith saying o Solomon that there's 'a toime to laugh un a toime to dance'.

Later that year the Star's opponents obtained the superficially damning evidence about the Star already referred to, from local boys imprisoned for theft. Sharples responded by enlisting the new Volunteer Force, including many of Bolton's Tory élite, for a performance of 'Othello' at the Theatre Royal.[10] In the music hall at the same time, however, while the sixpenny side boxes were full, the shilling centre boxes were 'often empty'. Nevertheless, Robert Greenhalgh remembered that the multiple establishment on the whole:

> was thoroughly well conducted, and it had a high reputation. Many of our greatest local dignitaries were amongst its patrons; even clergymen did not disdain to visit some sections of it.[11]

Of course, styles varied from one performance to another (especially if one was a special gala performance where local notables were invited), and from one time of the week to another. The Star on a Saturday evening, when workers of all classes would bring their wages and perhaps their wives to unwind after a week's labour, was probably very different from the Star on a 'Saint Monday' afternoon, part-filled with colliers and others spinning out their weekend in drink for as long as they could manage. As late as the 1920s the Grand, the resplendent successor to the Star/Museum, still opened on Monday afternoons, when the audiences were notoriously difficult; 'the artists . . . all felt that if their acts went well on Monday afternoons their reputations were enhanced for the whole week'.[12]

The 1872 Bolton Improvement Act gave the magistrates control over all licences for music, dancing, billiards and various other entertainments in the borough, whether in pubs or not, and there was an immediate squeeze on publicans who put on music and dancing. The Temperance Hall, Co-Operative Hall and Baths' Assembly Rooms were all allowed licences, but the Museum Music Hall was turned down without comment. The blow was harsh and unexpected, and local opinion was outraged that the Improvement Act could be used for 'the confiscation of property'. Faced with protest meetings, a petition of 1,800 citizens, the appearance of the Chief Constable and several of his officers as enthusiastic character witnesses for Weston and the Museum, and the threat of legal action, the magistrates relented, and granted all the disputed licences.[13] Their control of licensing still gave them effective powers of censorship, for even it they might have been defeated in the higher courts, they could still expensively interrupt the running of the Museum. Weston must have realised this, and trod a careful line between popularity and propriety, without sacrificing either when it really mattered. The 1875 pantomime 'Cinderella' was seen as a bawdy 'burlesque' when first presented to the packed New Year audience, but it was then rapidly made into 'a very decent entertainment' with 'several of the more objectionable portions . . . struck out' in time for the annual licensing session. However, the magistrates made it a condition of his licence that the words and music of all the songs to be performed each week were to be submitted to the Magistrates' Court every Monday morning. Even the encores were to be from previously approved material. In 1880 the management paid for a policeman to attend every night, although this did not cure the 'gallery gods' of the habit of spitting and dropping orange peel and other rubbish over other spectators.[14] Perhaps pressure from the authorities made Weston decide he had had enough; at any rate, he sold the whole complex in 1877 and emigrated to the USA, though not before leaving the town with another music hall to its name.

The Temple Opera House started life as a cotton mill in Dawes Street. Its extravagantly ugly design — it even had a dome — earned it the nick-name 'Solomon's Temple', and it was well-suited to being a music hall. Weston bought it up and converted it into a 5,000-capacity 'opera house', which opened on October 20th 1877, offering 'prices to the million' — 6d. to 'the whole of the gigantic pit' and 4d. to the gallery. He ran it for a short time before selling it and emigrating — a wise move, for it never really paid. Probably, its huge size made it expensive to run and uncomfortable to attend, and it fell into disuse as a theatre for two or three years, playing host to several Tory rallies. It was then sold to a Leeds maltster, and leased by Charles Majilton, the locally-known 'grotesque actor and pantomimist'. He optimistically renovated it, and extended the gallery, which brought the capacity up to an alleged 6,000. It re-opened on Christmas Eve 1881 with a pantomime, which was followed by several productions which thoroughly exploited the scope given by the sheer size of the place. In 'The Poor of London', for example, a great fire was depicted and a fully-equipped fire engine came dashing to the rescue, which caused great excitement, 'the audience rising nightly en masse'. Before the Temple had a chance to prove its viability, however, it was burnt down in April 1882 at a cost, only partly insured, of some £10,000; Majilton was ruined.[15]

The Temple, although it was ostensibly permanent, was in fact only a more ambitious version of the circus-style wooden pavilions, such as the 'Victoria Theatre' (or 'California Market') described above which had been providing Boltoners with entertainment outside the normal theatres and music halls for many years. Weston himself had been refused a licence for such a place in 1861, and one called the St. John's Pavilion was open in the 1860s, although it was strictly prevented from showing stage plays. Another wooden pavilion, called Pullan's Theatre of Varieties, was put up in the wholesale market in 1879. Pullan had been the lessee of the Museum Music Hall for the previous two years, and he took with him the Museum's compere, J. B. Geoghegan, to act as chairman. This seems to have been successful enough, for Pullan's remained in business for five or six years altogether.[16]

## Late Victorian Developments

The Theatre Royal and Museum Music Hall survived these years of competition well enough, despite some interruption in the continuity of management after the sale of the premises in 1877. The Theatre Royal was managed for some forty years from 1880 by J. F. Elliston, who had begun his career in the later 1870s by distinguishing himself as stage manager for the then owner, C. H. Duval. He rapidly rose to becoming sole proprietor and manager before going into partnership with J. Atkinson & Co. Ltd., a local brewing firm. J. B. Geoghegan was persuaded to return to the Museum Music Hall as manager, and from 1882 to 1887 he and Elliston ran the two places between them. The partnership with the brewery enabled Elliston to raise the capital to expand the Theatre Royal in 1886 (not long after the wooden 'Theatre of Varieties' on the wholesale market lapsed) into 'a first rate temple of the drama' which could accommodate 3,000 people. The stage alone was enlarged from 2,700 to 4,000 square feet — 1,500 people could have stood on it at once — so that it was well-suited to putting on the most spectacular of productions. On January 4th 1888, however, it was burnt down by a 'besotted half-imbecile bill-poster' who bore a grudge against it. (Theatre fires were clearly endemic in Bolton, but this one, fortunately, was the last.) The music hall next door was hardly touched, but even so the damage was estimated at £12,000.[17]

Elliston lost no time in having the Theatre rebuilt, and engaged his friend Frank Matcham, the most prolific theatre architect of the day, to draw up the plans. The actual construction work was done in an almost incredible twenty weeks and the new Theatre Royal was opened on November 19th, 1888. At 1,800, its capacity was less than before, but it made up for this in comfort and quality. It was decorated in 'the Moorish style' with marble staircases and a sumptuous dress circle which held 110. One of the four private boxes was designated 'The Mayor Box', to which the Mayor nominally had first refusal, and which he occupied on

68

the opening night. Even the pit had upholstered stalls (although they were reported to be cramped and draughty) but the 'pittites' were kept from the rest of the house by an elaborate system of barriers, 'crush rooms' and turnstiles. The 'gallery gods' were still further segregated, having a completely separate entrance at the side of the building. The emphasis on classiness paid off and Elliston had no difficulty in persuading the magistrates to grant him a drinks' licence for the place, and to allow him to open on Ash Wednesday — developments which he presented to them as part of the twin march of progress and respectability. The rapid and therefore cheap construction, combined with the relatively high prices (a 6d. gallery and a 1/– pit on the opening night), the large number of carefully protected expensive seats, and the profits from the bar, helped pay for the whole enterprise. Audiences were treated to an endless run of musical comedies, pantomimes, and Gilbert and Sullivan, another sign that middle-class tastes were being catered for. For Weston, courting respectability had been an occasional tactic to keep the magistrates sweet at the right times; for Elliston, it was a matter of economics.[18]

In August 1894 an extravagant new entertainment palace, the 'Grand Cirque' was opened in Churchgate. It eventually superseded the old Museum Music Hall (now the Victoria) which disappeared around 1897. The Grand was another of Matcham's designs, financed by the new Bolton Theatre and Entertainments Company Ltd. It was done up in 'French renaissance' style and seated 3,000 — more than its predecessor or the Theatre Royal. A unique feature was that the stage could be transformed into a sunken circus ring; hence the name 'Grand Cirque'. The idea may have come from the success of a wooden circus erected on the site in 1891; the Bolton Theatre and Entertainment Company bought it up and closed it in the following year. In fact, the ring was little used, but the episode does show that the old connection between circus, theatre and music hall still operated. The Grand was leased to George Scott of the Palace Theatre, Manchester, who intended to run it as a 'high-class music hall', but he failed to make a success of it and the management reverted to the Company. The emphasis on outward respectability remained, however, and the different sectors of the audience were kept just as carefully segregated as in the neighbouring theatre. The Cirque was used by the Bolton Amateur Operatic Society for their performances, and Elliston and his enterprises were very favourably written about in the local fireside temperance magazine, *Bolton Review*. The *Review* also carried an interview with Teddy Whittle, the local comedian, who played both the Grand and the Temperance Hall, and who disarmingly stated that:

> Most of the subjects of comic songs are: Girls, Booze, Rowdy Dowdy, Stay Out all Night, Jolly Good Spree, Run in, Up Before the Beak, Fined Forty Bob, & c. . . Anything vulgar and nasty is against my nature and bringing up.

Of course, Whittle had his Temperance audience to think of when he said this, but such an attitude is in keeping with the trend of late nineteenth-century music hall, where uniformed commissioners kept an eye on people as they queued, and where 'unduly vigorous [audience] participation was discouraged and even protracted

69

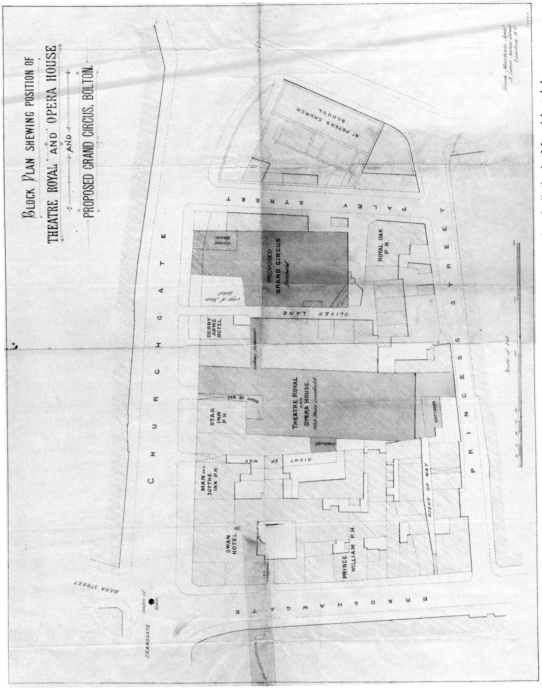

Fig. 13   J. F. Elliston's New Theatre Royal, Churchgate, sumptuously rebuilt 'in the Moorish style' in 1888. Frank Matcham drew up the plans in a matter of months, the building work took 22 weeks, and the theatre was re-opened only ten months after its predecessor was gutted by fire.

applause was sometimes frowned upon'. In containing the behaviour of music hall audiences, 'big business succeeded where social reformers failed'.[19]

However, there was another side to this. Performers developed skills of gesture and innuendo to protect their popularity against the censor. The texts of the songs to be performed were probably of little use to the magistrates, for a good performer could make a bawdy song sound innocent or a drawing-room ballad appear obscene; in any case, with the police among Weston's clients and supporters, the magistrates can have little control over what was actually said on the night. Two visitors from Oxford in the late 1890s felt that Lancashire's better-class music halls fostered an unhealthy hypocrisy with their reliance on prurient sensationalism and slick vulgarity; the inclusion of religious songs was often a sign that the rest of the programme was 'of a kind at which the spectator need not be prudish to wince'. Elliston himself was known in theatrical circles as 'a volatile young man' of 'Falstaffian proportions', fond of 'the gay life' on the Continent, but he certainly knew how to flatter and cajole magistrates — and Temperance campaigners. The audience may have been carefully segregated, but this was obviously necessary as far as middle-class spectators were concerned, for they were still not in themselves numerous enough for the Grand to be run as a purely 'high-class music hall'. And although the audience were now seated in close, orderly rows, rather than ranged round benches and tables, the various 'crush rooms' and smoking rooms still helped to keep Bolton's leading music hall a centre of weekend social life as well as simply a place of entertainment.[20]

The move up-market of the Star-Museum-Victoria-Grand did not, of course, mean that there had been a similarly far-reaching change in the cultural outlook of its original working-class audience. Below the 'high class' music hall there was a whole network of 'poor people's music halls' in Lancashire, visited and described in the late 1890s by two Oxford social explorers in an article which reads rather like a piece of Mass Observation forty years before its time. It is difficult to place any definite example of a 'poor people's music hall' in Bolton in the 1890s because both the press and such published reminiscences as exist concentrate on the Churchgate theatres and music halls. The poorer halls were small places, with a definite stage and either stall seating or tables and chairs for the customers. They were often run in connection with a pub, but they were separate from it and sold only non-alcoholic drinks. Apart from the lack of alcohol, the Star/Museum until the 1870s fitted this description; so too the earlier Millstone and Finley Frazer's 'Bird in Hand'. The young witnesses in Salford gaol mentioned others — 'The Craven Heifer, Benjamin Law's Bolton Moor' and 'Ben Lacy's . . . a hell place', while J. B. Geoghegan of the Museum Music Hall had earlier acted as master of ceremonies at the Ship Inn. The January 1873 licensing sessions was the first to be held under the 1872 Improvement Act, which required that all places of public music or dancing be licensed separately from any drinks licence they may have had. Apart from the Star/Museum, three other pubs had specially built singing rooms which needed licences of music and dancing, and another 14 pubs asked for licences for public music only. In addition, many other pubs had music on an irregular, informal basis, but did not need music licences because they did not advertise. After a failed attempt by the magistrates to cut down these numbers, the number of places — not all of them pubs — licensed for music rose to around 60 by 1880, with another dozen or so licensed for both music and dancing. Thereafter the numbers remained steady for the rest of the century; the stricter licensing of public houses in this period would have encouraged innkeepers to separate their potentially disorderly and disreputable entertainment rooms from their pubs.[21] We can, then, be reasonably confident that the sort of 'poor people's music halls' described by Russell and Campagnac, the Oxford visitors, existed in Bolton, just as in the rest of Lancashire. Their observations could equally apply to the Star and Museum earlier in the century and, indeed, have a bearing upon much of popular entertainment during our period.

The 'poor people's music halls', they found, were frequented not by the usual 1890s music hall audience of 'clerks or shop-keepers or shop-assistants' but by 'labourers, artisans, porters, navvies (and) street-sellers of all kinds'. During the entertainments:

> No effort of continuous thought is demanded from the spectators. Their attention is seized forcibly, their ears are filled, their eyes caught . . . There is little exercise in interpretation; everything is bold and plain and obvious . . .

Some of the songs were familiar from generations before (a similar comment had been made fifty years earlier); most, however, seemed to have been 'manufactured wholesale, like the tawdry imitations of jewels' worn by the singers, and brimmed over with sentiment or, more fashionably, shallow patriotism. The jokes concerned

> The foibles of the police, the swagger of the soldier, the imbecility of the fop; all kinds of bodily peculiarities . . . and some diseases . . . physical oddity is seized upon . . . because it stands for some quality of character, which is the real object of the ridicule . . .

The subject matter of comedy and sentiment alike were often strong — murder, torture, suffering, death, prison, poverty and 'the naked and hideous disruption of domestic happiness'. Conjuring tricks, acrobatics and especially dancing ('really clever, though far more violent than graceful') were among the favourite turns, as they had been at the Star/Museum, but these amusements were smoothly interleaved between the tragedy and comedy, murder and mayhem — rather like a modern television channel. The audience, thought Russell and Campagnac:

> do not recognise the possibility of any relation between one and another, and thus their laughter is genuine, their awe is real, their merriment is unaffected and their loyalty pure, though their minds are not delicately or intimately moved, nor their souls subtly or deeply stirred. The whole thing is honest and spontaneous, as far as it goes.

Without giving their subjects much credit for sophistication or independence of mind, the authors hit upon the differences between the entertainments at these threepenny halls and the more 'decent' but more prurient and innuendo-ridden offerings of the sixpenny and shilling variety theatres. The straightforward delights of the poor people's music halls seemed to be 'more wholesome' and 'of a higher order':

> The merriment provided by these entertainments is heartly and unaffected . . . the enjoyment is social . . . moral judgements, however grossly expressed, are yet formed . . . with almost entire unanimity . . . There is no affectation here, no pretence of liking what is not liked.

The brutal and (to relatively refined observers) upsetting content of the comic sketches was not crude or 'demoralising', thought Russell and Campagnac, i.e. cathartic — a 'safety valve' as the *Bowtun Loominary* had once described it — or a tonic. All these sensations, disappointments and miseries were part of the audience's own lives, and in laughing at them, for a time at least, they laughed at their own plight.

Middle-class observers were at last beginning to realise what J. T. Staton and his popular dialect papers had insisted all along: that the rough, untrained pleasures of the mass of the people were not born of viciousness or immorality; rather, they had their own respectability, although it could hardly be the 'Respectability' of people brought up in a more comfortable middle-class environment. The commercial success of the late nineteenth-century music hall mirrored an economic change rather than a cultural one — the increasing numbers of relatively well-off shopkeepers and assistants, skilled workers and clerks, the slowly rising standard of living for many other workers who were happy to spend money on seeing famous acts in elaborate theatres, and the fact the Bolton was now a town of some 150,000 people, much more able by its sheer size to support bigger entertainments than fifty years before. Not far beneath the Grand and the Royal, however, there were still dozens of small concert rooms, hundreds of pubs and thousands of homes, streets and workplaces where people met and entertained themselves. Popular culture in Bolton was far longer lasting and had far deeper roots than did the passing glitter of the extravagantly unlikely variety theatres which, over a few decades, gave the people a little space to play in.

*Notes*
1. This is a simplified account drawn from ambiguous evidence; for further detail, see Appendix; *BC* 30.12.1854, 16.7.1859, 10.3.1860, 22.2.1873, 17.3.1877; Star Museum catalogue/leaflet *c*.1859 cited in Chapter 6, note 2.
2. *BC* 1.1.1859; *BL* 1857, p. 183; *BWJ* 21.12.1872; *BC* 29.6.1872.
3. *BC* 30.12.1854; *BL* 13.1.1855.
4. *Depositions relating to the Star* (*BRL*) pp. 6, 8, 12, 2. The practice of selling drinks from the pit landing was stopped in 1859 because of the crush it caused ('Depositions . . .', p. 15).
5. *BC* 22.2.1873.
6. *BJG* 8.9.1914, 2.3.1928, 3.11.1933; a similar, unattributed account appears in Mellor, *Northern Music Hall*, p. 23.
7. *BC* 18.11.1854, 14.4.1855, 1.12.1855, 26.12.1857. This prejudice was presumably linked to the fact that Shakespeare was popular among the working class, as Douglas Reid has found in Birmingham (*Popular Theatre in Victorian Birmingham, loc. cit.*). Not all of it was a sort with which we would be familiar today; a good travelling fairground theatre could get through a full-length tragedy in twenty minutes, while in 1814 Bolton theatre offered favourite single acts from five of Shakespeare's plays, staged consecutively (playbill ND/40).

8. *BC* 28.2.1857; *BL* 22.1.1859; Bailey, *op. cit.*, pp. 153–4, 165–6.
9. 'A Chronological List of Bolton Theatres and Music Halls and their Managers 1868–1914, from Era Almanack' (*BRL*); *BC* 24.3.1900.
10. *BRL* playbills ZZ/82 1858/1; *BC* 15.1.1859, 7.4.1860, 30.6.1860; *BL* 22.1.1859.
11. 'Depositions' (1860), p. 12; Greenhalgh MSS.
12. 'Bolton's Homely Centre of Song and Laughter, by Quidnunc' (undated cutting (1954) on Grand Theatre, in *BRL*).
13. Bolton Improvement Act, 1872; *BC* 25.1.1873, 1.2.1873, 22.2.1873; Bailey, *op. cit.*, p. 162. The threat of legal action was not an 'idle threat' and may have been decisive; Weston's solicitor referred to a recent case of an Oldham music hall owner who had been similarly treated under the 1865 Oldham Improvement Act, but subsequently won a licence in Quarter Sessions. Two years later Weston's tenant in the Angel Inn, Robert Blake, took the local authorities to the High Courts and won the rescinding of a £100 fine on him for keeping a betting house, so the magistrates' powers seem to have been significantly limited in this area. (*BC* 23.10.1875.)
14. *BC* 23.1.1875, 29.1.1876; *BEN* 7.1.1880, 9.1.1880.
15. Greenhalgh MSS; *BC* 17.3.1877, 19.5.1877, 20.10.1877, 15.4.1882, 22.4.1882; *BWJ* 28.12.1872; *BJG* 10.10.1919.
16. *BC* 20.3.1869, 3.9.1861, 23.3.1878; 'A Chronological List of Bolton Theatres . . .'; *BJG* 26.1.1889 (in *BRL* cuttings book 1889–90, p. 21).
17. *BC* 7.1.1888; Records of John Atkinson and Co. Ltd. (PRO BT31/3042/17257).
18. *BC* 17.11.1888, 24.11.1888; Brian Walker (ed.), *Frank Matcham: Theatre Architect* (Belfast, 1980), pp. 7–9, 25, 28, 156. The pictures of the Theatre Royal and Grand on pages 3, 8, and 26 are all in *BRL* and contemporary Ordnance Survey maps provide further detail.
19. 'Bolton's Homely Centre of Mirth' (see note 12); *Bolton Review* 1897, pp. 38–9, 115; Walker, *op. cit.*, p. 29; Lesley Brain, 'Working-Class Leisure in Bolton 1885–1914' (Lancaster University M.A. dissertation, 1979), pp. 38–9; Peter Bailey's paper on 'The Working-Class and Leisure: Conference Report' in *Bulletin of the Society for the Study of Labour History 32* (Spring 1976), pp. 12–13.
20. *BC* 24.11.1888; Walker, *op. cit.*, pp. 7–8; C. E. B. Russell and E. T. Campagnac, 'Poor People's Music Halls in Lancashire', *Economic Review X* (1900), pp. 289–308 (published by the Oxford University branch of the Christian Social Union); Penelope Summerfield, 'The Effingham Arms and the Empire', pp. 224–34, in *Popular Culture and Class Conflict 1590–1914* (eds.) Eileen and Stephen Yeo (Brighton, 1981), pp. 209–40. I am also indebted for this point to Lois Rutherford's paper on 'Comic Singers and Music Hall Respectability' to the conference of the Social History Society at Chester in December 1981.
21. Russell and Campagnac, *op. cit.*; 'Depositions' (1860), pp. 4, 11; *BJG* 26.1.1889; *BC* 25.1.1873, 22.2.1873; Bolton Chief Constable's annual reports.

# Conclusion

'Old wine in new bottles' in an apt way of describing the growth of leisure in nineteenth-century Bolton. The 'wine' was the people; the 'bottles' were the factories, neighbourhoods, institutes, football grounds, music halls, and the physical fabric of the town generally. Unfortunately, it is much easier to collect old bottles than old wine — history, of necessity, is often more concerned with things and places, rather than with people directly. When looking at the growth of leisure, this can be misleading. One might look at the geometrically laid out housing of Bolton and the regular and relentless working weeks of most of its people, and then at the carefully marked-off parks and sports' grounds and the many recreations concentrated in the weekend; one might compare these and conclude that by 1900 leisure had assumed new forms which were tightly integrated with the demands of working life. In one sense, this was true; in another, it was not. As we have seen, those people who aimed at a thorough-going modern reform of recreation found that even their successes did not turn out how they expected. Football was introduced by the middle class, but in the end, after furious arguments, working-class professionalism and partisanship rather than the ideals of 'rational athleticism' came to dominate it. The big music halls at the end of the century put on a respectable face, but their managers and performers developed new professional skills which allowed them to keep on many of their old bawdy ways, and there still remained a whole layer of pubs and cheap music halls which catered for unreformed working-class tastes. Working men's clubs were founded amid high expectations about the growth of sober and decent recreations, but through popular demand (or, rather, lack of it) they were forced to become similar to pubs. New leisure institutions of all kinds had to adapt themselves to existing popular taste — in short, we find old wine in new bottles.

This study has stressed continuity rather than change in popular leisure, and its main weakness has perhaps been not paying enough attention to the other side of working-class social life — the 'culture of improvement'. In a much-quoted commentary, Samuel Bamford, the radical weaver, wrote of the people of Lancashire in the 1840s:

> They are the greatest readers; can show the greatest number of good writers; the greatest number of sensible and considerate public speakers. They can show a greater number of botanists; a greater number of horticulturalists, a greater number who are acquainted with the abstruse sciences; the greatest number of poets, and a greater number of good musicians, whether choral or instrumental.[1]

Similarly, Richard Guest, a Lancashire commentator, in 1823:

> The Athletic exercises of Quoits, Wrestling, Foot-ball, Prison-bars and Shooting with the Long-bow are become obsolete . . . they are now Pigeon-fanciers, Canary-breeders and Tulip-growers . . .[2]

The working-class self-improvers appear in our story now and again — in the

Chartist Institute designed, among other things, to lure people away from the Star Inn and Finley Frazer's, or in the party of working men who approached the public librarian to complain that the books in the reference library 'were not of a sufficiently high character for them' and request more of Gibbon and Macauley. But, judging by the small numbers actually enrolled at the Mechanics' Institute and even the most famous of the mill institutes, such people were a small minority. 'Respectability' became in time a part of the general run of working-class life — not through improving institutions or rational recreation, but in other ways. Best clothes were worn far more often to the pub on Saturday night or at wakes and fairs than they were to church or to quiet evenings of 'sober and sensible' amusement. Indeed, the mixing of riotousness and respectability was best seen in public holidays, and one such local event which persisted well into the twentieth century illustrates these various themes — the custom of the mock Mayor of Ringley.

The ceremony took place on the first Sunday in May, on the day after the anniversary sermons were preached at St. Saviour's church, during what had become known as Ringley Wakes. Staging 'mock mayor' type ceremonies is an ancient custom, dating back to the middle ages, but this particular one probably began in the second quarter of the nineteenth century in what was already an industrial village. It still flourished in the face of some adversity in the early part of this century, and only finally died out in the 1930s.[3]

On the appointed day, the customers at the Horse Shoe Inn, Ringley, would elect as 'Lord Mayor' from amongst themselves 'the man who could drink the most beer'. He was then formally proclaimed in a speech by a man styling himself for the occasion the Lord Mayor's clerk, which drew attention to the ancient origin of the custom beyond living memory, detailed the privileges of the Lord Mayor, and also laid down some of his obligations, such as being lenient with anyone found drunk. The Mayor then read a list of the sports to be played and their prizes — bowling sweeps, pigeon flying, quoiting, foot racing, jumping, swarming the pole, grinning through a horse collar, singing, dancing and general merrymaking — and called for three cheers for the Lady Mayoress, the landlords and the landladies. Most of these sports were no longer played; only the bowls and the pigeon flying, probably later additions on the list, were put on by publicans in 1905, for example. The Mayor was then carried shoulder high on a form, wearing a smart military-style braided jacket and shako hat, with a piece of bread on the end of a toasting fork as his symbol of office. The party toured anything up to nineteen pubs from Ringley to Stoneclough Brow, accompanied by a raucous band and a noisy retinue, finishing up at the old canal bridge Ringley. Here, the Mayor read his speech again, even though he was very much the worse for wear and would often have fallen off his form several times by then — the need for a man who could hold his drink became obvious. He was then tipped in the canal, and dragged out by several helpers. Parents and Sunday school teachers tried to keep their children away from these goings-on, but in vain; the custom caused great excitement locally, and the final ceremony always drew a large crowd.

76

There was, however, a more respectable side to the custom. For the rest of the year, the Lord Mayor of Ringley was entitled to a pint of beer, a pipe of tobacco and a match every Sunday in each of the three pubs in the village — the Crown, the Lord Nelson, and the Horse Shoe — but only on condition that he turned up in his best clothes, clean and tidy and sober, having first been to the local church. According to custom, the vicar could not refuse him entry. The custom upheld standards as well as temporarily mocking them. Since the biggest drinker was chosen, it may also have helped to bring him to order in a way which gave offence to no-one and thus kept the community together in support of mutual values. These values allowed both riotousness and respectability to have their place. In fact, neither the Mayor-making day nor the Mayor's Sunday behaviour during the rest of the year were wholly one or the other. The proclamation of the new Mayor enjoined him to be lenient with drunks, but also stated that he should continue to prosecute thieves and burglars. The Mayor's Sunday duties, however, did not preclude his getting drunk later — indeed, three free pints gave him a good start. His privileges also included

> one grand privilege allowed him which has rarely if ever been extended to any Mayor in the land besides himself, and this is this. If the Lord Mayor goes home drunk and his wife turns him out, and he has nowhere to go, if he sees three pigs asleep in a midden he can drive the middle pig out and lay down in its warm place betwixt the other two, and woe be to than man if he resides within the boundary of the borough of Ringley who dares to dispute his worship's authority.

This sort of thing was hardly a serious challenge to the authorities, but it did uphold traditional values which were no longer generally approved of by those in authority, particularly the right to uninhibited alcoholic pleasures.

Speculating about its origin may give us a further clue to what the custom of the Lord Mayor of Ringley was about. The Lord Mayor and his colleagues were usually colliers, and Ringley's colliers were noted for their conservatism. Yet (according to the proclamation in 1894) the custom seems to have originated in a burlesque of the activities of a certain bleachworks owner called Gresham who, on the Monday after St. Saviour's anniversary sermons, would parade through his works and the rest of the village dressed in a 'uniform'. Ringley's millowners were noted for their radicalism, which was shared by their men, so perhaps this custom began as a good-humoured attack by conservative colliers on the pretensions of radical millowners.

The disorderliness of the Mayor-making made it unpopular with the landlord of the Horse Shoe in the early years of this century, although the Cross Keys and the Lord Nelson, which were not quite at the centre of the festivities, still put on bowling and pigeon flying to attract custom. The custom continued in defiance of the landlord of the Horse Shoe one year, but then went into disgrace for a time after the Mayor assaulted the vicar. None the less, it revived to continue into the nineteenth-thirties, when it underwent a final crisis. The day was still dreaded at this time by the daughter of the landlord of the Lord Nelson but the Mayor-making.

was losing steam. By that time, Outwood Colliery had closed, and one year no collier could be found to act as Mayor. Eventually, one of the showmen up for the wakes agreed to take part, but only on condition that he was christened with a bucket of water rather than total immersion. He could hardly have turned up for his beer and tobacco every Sunday; the last mayor, however, was a local man, Billy Pilkington, in the mid-nineteen-thirties.

The modern industrial village of Ringley, then, supported for about a century a custom which had all the features of what are usually regarded as pre-industrial festivals — it was a period of temporary licence and merry-making, but it upheld rather than challenged the values of the community involved. Ringley itself had many 'pre-industrial' characteristics: it was stable and close-knit, full of people who had lived there all their lives, who all knew each other, and who were probably related as well. Elizabeth Whittaker's parents were regarded as outsiders decades after they first arrived in the area: 'the Ringleyites were very, very, clannish, were the Ringleyites'. That a 'traditional' type society such as this could grow up and create its own 'ancient' customs in the depths of industrial Lancashire shows the dangers of thinking too closely in terms of 'industrial' and 'pre-industrial' societies, or of assuming that working in modern industry necessarily

Fig. 14   Allen Clarke ('Teddy Ashton'), the Bolton radical and dialect writer, on holiday in the Fylde. Clarke loved the countryside and disliked the grimy town where he had been born, but he did his best to brighten the lives of its ordinary inhabitants with his humorous writings, and holidays were always a favourite topic.

78

changed people's taste for leisure. Nor was the commonly-used distinction between 'respectable' and 'rough' pastimes a clear one; Ringley's mock Mayor-making custom smoothly combined both elements.

In Bolton as a whole, there had none the less clearly been great changes in leisure over the nineteenth century. Viewed from a distance, the town's society, for all its subtle social details, appeared as a well-defined class society, where social class and different recreations went together. This was how Allen Clarke, the Bolton socialist and author of the leisure magazine 'Teddy Ashton's Journal', saw Bolton at the end of the 1890s:

> Broadly, the whole population of the town may be divided into three castes . . . The first caste, consisting of employers, clergymen, solicitors, physicians, tradesmen on a large scale, dwells in wide sub-urban streets, made respectably natural with a few trees, inhabiting villas, semi-detached and single, shopping at the big stores (in the day-time, having first choice of everything), drinking at the best hotels, occupying the front seats at the more select concerts, the boxes, the stalls, and the dress circle of the theatre, front cushioned seats nearest the pulpit at church or chapel, buying magazines in addition to newspapers, and having pictures, book-cases, and wine-cellars of their own, and often private carriages.

> The second caste is composed of the best-paid clerks, book-keepers, managers, and the better sort of working folks; they live in streets narrower than those of caste one, have no trees, drink their beer at smaller hotels, buy food and drink at the smaller stores (or maybe the Co-operative Society), use the pit of the theatre, the middle and rear pews of the church, buy a newspaper or two, have a few cheap pictures on the walls (the inevitable oil-portrait of the head of the family and his spouse), get books from the public library, perhaps buy a few of their own, and walk, or use the tram.

> The third caste is made up of "labourers" and poorer workmen; they live in small houses, — all joined and jammed together to save space and make more rents for the landlord — in narrow streets; they shop at the smallest and dirtiest shops, they drink in low taverns, we find pawnshops numerous in their localities, they get their music in hideous singing rooms, they sit in the gallery at the theatre, they have no books, no church, no art.

> Beneath these, there is a fourth caste; but these cannot be classified, for they cannot afford even a bury-hole for cemetery classification.[4]

Allen Clarke's description here omits a great deal — not least sport, and clubs and societies — but it does indicate how lifestyle and leisure went together. The rise of mass commercial leisure towards the end of the nineteenth century was very striking (to a modern observer, if not to Allen Clarke) but it is easy to lose sight of the simple fact that most people's leisure was not bought and consumed, in the modern way; it was home-made. Leisure in the home has hardly been touched upon in this study, through simple lack of evidence, but it was undoubtedly significant, particularly among the middle-classes whose more comfortable homes were the scene of all sorts of domestic pastimes, such as music, sewing, crafts, reading, writing and entertaining. For the working-class, the pub still dominated leisure time, performing broadly similar functions as a hundred years before. Clubs and societies, often organised around pubs and by their members, provided a great deal of recreation — friendly societies, sports' clubs and leagues, youth clubs, holiday clubs and the rest. Even where amusement was simply paid for, as in going to a football match or a music hall, much of the enjoyment was social. Although circumstances and details changed very much over the century, the story was much the same throughout; wherever they could, people made their own leisure.

Fig. 15    The Lord Mayor of Ringley reading the proclamation outside the Horse Shoe.

*Notes*
1.    Samuel Bamford, *Walks in South Lancashire* (Blackley, 1844), pp. 13–14; Bailey, *op. cit.*, pp. 10–11.
2.    Richard Guest, *A Compendious History of the Cotton Manufacture* (Manchester, 1823, rep. London, 1968), pp. 38–9.
3.    The church at Ringley, which dated originally from 1625, was rebuilt in 1826 and again in 1844. Presumably the anniversary sermons began at one or other of these rebuildings. The festival was almost certainly not a 'true' wakes; wakes in Lancashire always occur in late summer or early autumn and mark the dedication day of the church, and the anniversary sermon was a more modern invention, usually carefully distanced from the old wakes time. The sources for this account of Ringley Mayor-making are: transcript of the proclamation of the Mayor, 1894, taken from the original in the Horse Shoe Inn, Ringley; Elizabeth Whittaker, 'I Shall Never Forget the Day' (typescript); interview with Mrs Whittaker by Barry Mills, *BRL* tape 3B (partial transcript also in *BRL*); interview with Mrs Whittaker by Robert Poole (copy to be placed in *BRL*); slides and photos of Ringley Mayor-making, with commentary in *BRL*; interview with Arthur Kirkby, April 1973; North-West Sound Archive, tape 1979, no. 056; *BJG* 19.5.1905, 'An Old Custom Dies'; *The Archer* (n.d. but 1904–5), pp. 29–31, 'Lord Mayor of Ringley'; Haslam, *Our Lancashire Village*, pp. 17–18, 29–30.
4.    Allen Clarke, *Effects on the Factory System* (London, 1899), pp. 32–3.

# Appendix
## Bolton Theatres and Music Halls and their Managers

This is intended as a piece of social history, rather than theatre history. It has glossed over the vexatious, and even confounding, question, of exactly what theatres and music halls there were on the Star's Churchgate site, and who owned them. The question of how far and how early the Star was a 'true music hall' is addressed in note 3 to Chapter 6. This appendix is about buildings and managers.

The rebuilt Star Inn in 1855 began with one concert hall, called simply 'the Star'. By 1857, there were two places of entertainment there: the 'Star Theatre' (with a 4*d*. gallery and a 6*d*. pit) and the 'Star Music Hall' (admission by refreshment ticket). The 'Star Theatre' soon became the 'Theatre Royal' (a name which Sharples also applied to the Old Theatre in Mawdsley Street when he was leasing it at the time); the 'Star Music Hall' was usually advertised simply as the 'Concert Room, Churchgate'.[1] The Theatre Royal put on stage plays, so presumably Sharples obtained permission from the magistrates for this, but no record of a licence has been traced. Although the museum exhibition was re-established in 1858, the Star Music Hall/Concert Room did not become the 'Museum Music Hall' until some time in the 1860s.

Once these extensions were over, the Star had a change of management. William Sharples had taken over from his father, Thomas, in 1850. He was still 'a young man' in 1852, but seems to have given up managing his property in 1860. His name last appears in an advert in October of 1860, but no obituary had been found for him, and he may have continued as owner until 1873.[2]

His successor was James Pitney Weston, an actor and theatre company manager well known in Bolton and Manchester. He first leased the Theatre Royal from Sharples in the Autumn of 1860, and soon took over the rest of the site; in 1873 he said he had occupied the Museum Music Hall 'for ten years'.[3] Robert Greenhalgh remembered that he brought the premises from William Sharples's executors, but gave no date. According to a later account, this happened in 1873, when Weston outbid a Methodist minister to take the place for £4,500; the price was low because the lease was only for ten years.[4]

The narrative has been written, to avoid confusion, as if there were only two places of public music on the Churchgate site in this period: a Theatre Royal and a Star/Museum Music Hall. In fact, there was almost certainly for a time a third place — a smaller pub/concert hall. The *Era Almanack* from 1868 to 1871 lists a Theatre Royal, a Museum Music Hall, and a Star Music Hall. The magistrates' hearings for the granting of music licences in 1873 were told that the Museum Music Hall was connected to the Angel Inn. The Star Inn also applied for a music licence, but no separate music hall for that was mentioned. The Museum was stated at the time to be 'the only legitimate music hall in the borough'. The premises when sold in 1877 consisted of the Theatre Royal, Museum Music Hall, Star Inn and Angel Inn.[5]

The witnesses from Salford House of Correction in 1860 are not very useful in clearing up this puzzle, for they refer to the whole place indiscriminately as 'the Star'; clearly, there were two places of music there, and they seem to have shared much of the same audience. It seems possible that one was used as a theatre at some time and as a music hall at others. It is not always clear exactly what these and other contemporary descriptions refer to, but it is hoped that the arrangement of evidence used in Chapter 7 has not distorted the social history of the place.[6]

In March 1877 the whole complex was sold to a Mr Chaplin, who was then renting the Theatre Royal for £500 a year. The price was £11,500, but there was a mix-up. Chaplin defaulted, and it later went to a consortium of three businessmen for £8,450. The next few years saw several different managers at the Theatre and Museum. The long-time master of ceremonies at the Museum, J. B. Geoghegan, left for a time to own and conduct the wooden Theatre of Varieties on the wholesale market, but later returned to the Museum as Manager; he died in 1889.[7] From 1879 until death in 1882, C. H. Duval was listed as manager of the Theatre. From 1875 his stage manager was J. F Elliston, who later took over from Duval as manager. According to *Era Almanack* this was in 1882, but Brian Walker states that he actually took over when Duval retired in 1878.[8]

In 1880–2 the Museum was demolished, rebuilt to accommodate 2,500 people, and renamed the Victoria Variety Theatre. By this time a local brewery, John Atkinson and Company Ltd., were involved with the enterprise, but the sources conflict on the exact details of this.[9] The venture was clearly profitable, for Atkinson's nominal capital rose from £25,000 on its formation in 1882 (with only £8,864 initially taken up) to £50,000 in 1890 and £75,000 in 1891. Atkinson's was absorbed in 1895 by another local brewery company, Boardman's, specially formed for the purpose.

In 1889, after the rebuilding of the Theatre Royal, a new company, the Bolton Theatre and Entertainments' Company Ltd., was formed; unfortunately, none of its records survive in the PRO. By 1897 the company owned a whole stretch of Churchgate including the Theatre Royal (whose gross estimated annual rental was £354 — £146 less than it actually had been in 1877), the 1894 Grand Cirque (£780) and the Victoria Theatre of Varieties (£250).[10] The 1896 Ordnance Survey map still shows a small 'concert tavern' nestling in the front corner of the 'Proposed Grand Circus', while the old Star Inn still adjoined the Theatre Royal, although the two were now almost certainly separate.

Through all this opulent growth, backed by Limited Liability capital, J. F. Elliston remained in control of developments, staying with the Grand and Theatre Royal until his death on Christman Eve, 1920. He was also running the Theatre Royal in Blackburn in the 1880s, and became firm friends with the famous theatre architect Frank Matcham, who designed first the Blackburn theatre and then the two in Bolton for Elliston. Matcham also had it in his favour that the owner of the Bolton Theatre Royal in 1888 was F. W. Purcell, the son-in-law of Matcham's colleague, William Revill.[11]

To complete the story, Bolton acquired another music hall, the Empire Theatre of Varieties, which opened in August 1908 and became the Hippodrome. It was put by an experienced Rochdale manager, Thomas Hargreaves, but it too was bought up by the Bolton Theatre and Entertainments Company in 1915. It became a cinema in 1923, and the Theatre Royal followed suit in 1929, only a year after it was rebuilt as a theatre; the invention of talkies probably caused this change of policy. Both the Grand and the Theatre Royal were demolished in Spetember 1963.[12]

There is clearly plenty of room for theatre and music hall enthusiasts to do more detailed research on the rather confused and neglected musical history of Bolton. Most of the material on which this study is based is available in Bolton Reference Library, including photocopies of major newspaper reports.

*Notes*

1. *BC* 28.3.1857, 11.4.1857.
2. *Bolton Almanack* 1850, p. xv shows William Sharples as proprietor. His father's account book ends in January 1850.
3. *BC* 6.10.1860, 10.11.1861, 16.3.1861, 18.5.1861, 22.2.1873.
4. *BJG* 3.11.1933; *BC* 19.5.1877; Greenhalgh MSS.
5. 'A chronological list of Bolton theatres and music halls and their managers' (*BRL*); *BC* 25.1.1873, 22.2.1873, 17.3.1877, 19.5.1877.
6. E.g. 'Depositions' (1860), p. 2.
7. *BC* 17.3.1877, 19.5.1877, 20.8.1877; *BJG* 26.1.1889, 3.11.1933.
8. 'A chronological list'; Walker, *op. cit.*, p. 9; *BC* 7.1.1888.
9. Records of John Atkinson and Company Limited, PRO BT31/3042/17257; *BJG* 16.1.1889, 3.11.1933; 'A chronological list'.
10. *Bolton Rate Book*, 1897.
11. *Theatre Notebook* XXV, p. 155; Walker, *op. cit.*, pp. 7–9.
12. *BJG* 1.10.1937; Walker, *op. cit.*, p. 156.